# Data science from scratch

Ultimate guide to master Data Mining and Data-Analytic from linear algebra and statistics to practical examples of neural networks and machine learning in python

**[Ramon Base]**

1

## Legal & Disclaimer

The information contained in this book and its contents is not designed to replace or take the place of any form of medical or professional advice; and is not meant to replace the need for independent medical, financial, legal or other professional advice or services, as may be required. The content and information in this book has been provided for educational and entertainment purposes only.

The content and information contained in this book has been compiled from sources deemed reliable, and it is accurate to the best of the Author's knowledge, information and belief. However, the Author cannot guarantee its accuracy and validity and cannot be held liable for any errors and/or omissions. Further, changes are periodically made to this book as and when needed. Where appropriate and/or necessary, you must consult a professional (including but not limited to your doctor, attorney, financial advisor or such

# Table of Contents

# Book Description

Data is an important resource. However, if you do not have the right means to process it, then there is not much that you can benefit from regarding its value. Data Science is one of those multidisciplinary areas whose major focus is to derive value from data in all means. This book will explore the field of Data Science using data and its structure. In addition, it will describe high-level processes that one uses to change data into value.

You know that Data Science is a process. However, this does not mean that it lacks creativity. In fact, when you move deep into the stages of processing data, right from munging data sources to Machine Learning and finally data visualization, you will start to see that complex steps are involved in working with raw data.

The steps that one follows in transforming raw data into value also vary. For instance, in an explanatory analysis, you may have a cleaned data set that is ready to be imported into R, and you visualize the result but don't deploy the model.

Data comes in different forms, but at an advanced level, it exists in three major categories. Those categories are structured, semi-structured, and unstructured. Data Scientists are experts responsible for gathering, analyzing and interpreting large amounts of data to help businesses and organizations. Throughout all the chapters in this book, you are going to learn what the best Data Scientists know about Data Analytics, Machine learning, Big Data, Data Mining, and Statistics. Since Data Science is a multidisciplinary field, this book covers very critical concepts that you must know to become a Professional Data Scientist.

# Introduction

Data is a word that is known to us. When we place it into the right words, it is an accumulation of data that can be converted into a structure that can be prepared by PCs. In reality, there are two sorts of data, one that is comprehensible and the other that is machine readable. With regards to data science, machine-readable data is the one that we looked for. Tools help us process data and reveal things that can't be seen by a human. It is, in reality, a higher amount of an all-encompassing piece of data examination. It utilizes a ton of speculations and strategies of insights and other stuff to its utilization. These calculations and procedures are being used to extract knowledge and bits of knowledge of data. It helps organizations and brands a great deal in business related exercises. With the utilization of data science, it encourages these organizations to draw near to the clients guaranteeing better commitment. It causes them in arranging stuff and discuss things with the administration over arranging and organization.

Data researcher abilities and applications

Data Scientist is an individual who knows the proper tools and procedures of Data Science to influence data to produce more esteem. His or her obligations incorporate making various machine learning based tools or conventional methods to get the approved yield. One significant range of abilities that a data researcher should know is the knowledge of suitable programming systems. R writing computer programs is substantial for that since R is a standard language with regards to data dealing with orders. Likewise, Hadoop is another essential application for massive data investigation that is utilized a ton in this area. The specialized aptitudes are as significant as the nonspecialized ones. The most notable of the non-specialized abilities is communication without a doubt. Being a data researcher, it's imperative to comprehend the customer's needs and afterward chip away at it. This would decrease time, vitality, and eventually heaps of cash. Additionally, cooperation and other delicate abilities are significant while dealing with a significant undertaking, particularly in data examination.

Data Science and why it is fascinating?

Presently you may think for what reason to pick data science as a profession. The best thing about data science is the way that it is practically present anyplace. For instance, when you open your web crawler, everything works with proficient utilization of data science. Seeking through your question and after that, getting precisely the required outcome is a straightforward case of the size of data science. The various destinations that show you suggested frameworks or the computerized advertisements that are such an enormous amount of dependent on what you see on the web indicates how productive this data framework has progressed toward becoming. In the meantime, there is a lot of prospects for development in this part. Individuals are as yet hoping to make the mining and preparing states to be progressively streamlined, and after that, there is dependably space for something new. Another calculation, or another method for preparing, I mean it very well may be anything. It merely needs intrigued individuals.

Why Is Data Science Widely Used?

The upset of Data Science has changed the world with its considerable effect. It is an investigation of data or data, what it speaks to, from where it is gotten, and how to change it into an essential strategy while detailing business and IT approach. It is considered as the most excellent resource by each association in the present focused world.

It is one of the fields that discover applications crosswise over the various business, including communication, fund, fabricating, human services, retail, and so on.

The social insurance businesses have profited by Data Science as it makes practical treatment issues, demonstrative, quit checking, for example, authoritative facility costs and a general expense for human services. It has been a fantastic weapon for fighting diabetes, various heartsickness, and malignancy.

The data science gives an immense chance to the budgetary firm to rehash the business. In account, the use of data science is Automating Risk Management, Predictive Analytics, Managing client data, Fraud identification, Real-time Analytics, Algorithmic exchanging, Consumer Analytics.

In the assembling area, it can be utilized from various perspectives since the organizations are in need to locate the most recent arrangements and use cases for this data. It has likewise been helpful to the assembling organizations as it accelerates execution and creates a substantial scale process.

The space of retail has proliferated. It causes the retailer to oversee data and make a mental image of the client to gain proficiency with their sore focuses. Along these lines, this trap utilized by the retailer will, in general impact the client effectively.

Sorts of Jobs Offered in Data Science.

The interest of people with exceptional abilities in this field is high and will keep on expanding. Data Science experts are contracted by the greatest names in the business that are slanted to pay enormous compensation to talented experts. The kinds of occupations include:

Data Scientist: A data researcher is somebody who decodes large measures of data and extracts importance to support an association or organization to improve its activities. They utilize various tools, philosophies, insights, systems, calculations, etc. to examine data additionally.

Business Intelligent Analyst: In request to check the present status of an organization or where it stands, a Business Analyst utilizes data and searches for examples, business patterns, connections and concocts a representation and report.

Data Engineer: A data engineer likewise works with a comprehensive volume of data cleans, extracts, and makes advanced calculations for data business.

Data Architect: Data Architect works with framework creators, clients, and designers to keep up and ensure data sources.

Machine Learning Engineer: A machine learning engineer works with various calculations identified with machine learning like grouping, choice trees, characterization, arbitrary backwoods, etc.

What are the necessities to be a Data Science proficient?

In the IT business, the instructive prerequisites of data science are abrupt. Data Scientist position interest for cutting edge degrees like Master's qualification, Ph.D. or MBA. A few organizations will acknowledge a four-year college education in Computer Science, Engineering and Hard Science, Management Information System, Math and Statistics, Economics. Data Science assets are additionally accessible on the web, and some instructive suppliers likewise offer internet preparing of the course. This preparation focus on the innovations and aptitudes required to be a data researcher like Machine learning, SAS, Tableau, Python, R, and some more.

# Chapter 1: What Is Big Data

The arrival of Big Data resulted in the expansion of storage space. As a result, storage became the biggest hurdle to most enterprises. Besides this, both organizations and enterprises are required to build a framework and develop a solution to store data. Therefore, Hadoop and other frameworks were developed to solve this problem. Once this issue was solved, the focus shifted to how data could be processed. When it comes to data processing, it is hard not to talk about Data Science. That is why it is important to understand what Data Science is and how it can add value to a business.

Why is Data Science Important?

Traditionally, data was structured in a small size. This means that there was no problem if you wanted to analyze data. Why? There were simple BI tools that you could use to analyze data. But modern data is unstructured and different from traditional data. Therefore, you need to have advanced methods of data analysis. The image below indicates that before the year 2020, more than 80% of the data will be unstructured.

This data comes from different sources such as text files, financial logs, sensors, multimedia forms, and instruments. Simple BI tools cannot be used to process this kind of data as a result of the massive nature of data. For this reason, complex and advanced analytical tools and processing algorithms are required. These types of tools help a Data Scientist analyze and draw important insights from data.

There are still other reasons why Data Science has increasingly become popular. Let's take a look at how Data Science is applied in different domains.

Have you ever thought of having the ability to understand the exact requirements of your customers from existing data such as purchase history, past browsing history, income, and age? The truth is: now it is possible. There are different types of data which you can use to effectively train models and accurately recommend several products to customers.

Let's use a different example to demonstrate the role of Data Science in decision making. What if your car is intelligent enough to drive you home? That would be cool. Well, that is how the self-driving cars have been designed to work.

These cars gather live data from sensors to build a map of the surroundings. Based on this data, the car can make decisions such as when to slow down, when to overtake, and when to take a turn. These cars have complex Machine Learning algorithms that analyze the data collected to develop a meaningful result.

Data Science is further applied in predictive analytics. This includes places such as weather forecasting, radars, and satellites. Models have been created that will not only forecast weather but also predict natural calamities. This helps an individual to take the right measures beforehand and save many lives. The infographic presented below shows domains where Data Science is causing a big impact.

# Chapter 2: Operations on data

## Data Munging, cleaning, manipulating and rescaling data

Now that you've gone through a Python programming crash course and you have some idea of the basic concepts behind programming, we can start discussing the data science process.

So what does "data munging" even mean? A few decades ago, a group of MIT students came up with this term. Data munging is about changing some original data to more useful data by taking very specific steps. This is basically the data science pipeline. You might sometimes hear about this term being referred to as data preparation, or sometimes even data wrangling. Know that they are all synonyms.

In this chapter we're going to discuss the data science process and learn how to upload data from files, deal with missing data, as well as manipulate it.

The Process

All data science projects are different one way or another, however they can all be broken down into typical stages. The very first step in this process is acquiring data. This can be done in many ways. Your data can come from databases, HTML, images, Excel files, and many other sources, and uploading data is an important step every data scientist needs to go through. Data munging comes after uploading the data, however at the moment that raw data cannot be used for any kind of analysis. Data can be chaotic, and filled with senseless information or gaps. This is why, as an aspiring data scientist, you solve this problem with the use of Python data structures that will turn this data into a data set that contains variables. You will need these data sets when working with any kind of statistical or machine learning analysis. Data munging might not be the most exciting phase in data science, but it is the foundation for your project and much needed to extract the valuable data you seek to obtain.

In the next phase, once you observe the data you obtain, you will begin to create a hypothesis that will require testing. You will examine variables graphically, and come up with new variables. You will use various data science methodologies such as machine learning or graph analysis in order to establish the most effective variables and their parameters. In other words, in this phase you process all the data you obtain from the previous phase and you create a model from it. You will undoubtedly realize in your testing that corrections are needed and you will return to the data munging phase to try something else. It's important to keep in mind that most of the time, the solution for your hypothesis will be nothing like the actual solution you will have at the end of a successful project. This is why you cannot work purely theoretically. A good data scientist is required to prototype a large variety of potential solutions and put them all to the test until the best course of action is revealed.

One of the most essential parts of the data science process is visualizing the results through tables, charts, and plots. In data science, this is referred to as "OSEMN", which stands for "Obtain, Scrub, Explore, Model, Interpret". While this abbreviation doesn't entirely illustrate the process behind data science, it captures the most important stages you should be aware of as an aspiring data scientist. Just keep in mind that data munging will often take the majority of your efforts when working on a project.

Importing Datasets with pandas

Now is the time to open the toolset we discussed earlier and take out pandas. We need pandas to first start by loading the tabular data, such as spreadsheets and databases, from any files. This tool is great because it will create a data structure where every row will be indexed, variables kept separate by delimiters, data can be converted, and more.

We start by important pandas and naming our file. In the third line we can define which character should be used a separator with the "sep" keyword, as well as the decimal character with the "decimal" keyword. We can also specify whether there's a header with the "header" keyword, which in our case is set to none. The result of what we have so far is an object that we named "iris" and we refer to it as a pandas DataFrame. In some ways it's similar to the lists and dictionaries we talked about in Python, however there are many more features. You can explore the object's content just to see how it looks for now by typing the following line:

In: iris.head()

As you can see, we aren't using any parameters with these commands, so what you should get is a table with only the first 5 rows, because that's the default if there are no arguments. However, if you want a certain number of rows to be displayed, simply type the instruction like this:

iris.head(3)

Now you should see the first three rows instead. Next, let's access the column names by typing:

In: iris.columns

Out: Index(['sepal_length', 'sepal_width', 'petal_length', 'petal_width', 'target'], dtype='object')

The result of this will be a pandas index of the column names that looks like a list. Let's extract the target column. You can do it like this:

In: Y = iris['target']

Y

Out:

0Iris-setosa

1Iris -setosa

2Iris -setosa

3Iris -setosa

...

149Iris-virginica

Name: target, dtype: object

For now it's important only to understand that Y is a pandas series. That means it is similar to an array, but in this case it's one directional. Another thing that we notice in this example is that the pandas Index class is just like a dictionary index. Now let's type the following:

In: X = iris[['sepal_length', 'sepal_width']]

All we did now was asking for a list of columns by index. By doing so, we received a pandas dataframe as the result. In the first example, we received a one dimensional pandas series. Now we have a matrix instead, because we requested multiple columns. What's a matrix? If your basic math is a bit rusty, you should know that it is an array of numbers that are arranged in rows and columns.

Next, we want to have the dimensions of the dataset:

In: print (X.shape)

Out: (150, 2)

In:  print (Y.shape)

Out: (150,)

What we have now is a tuple. We can now see the size of the array in both dimensions. Now that you know the basics of this process, let's move on to basic preprocessing.

Preprocessing Data with pandas

The next step after learning how to load datasets is to get accustomed to the data preprocessing routines. Let's say we want to apply a function to a certain section of rows. To achieve this, we need a mask. What's a mask? It's a series of true or false values (Boolean) that we need to tell when a certain line is selected. As always, let's examine an example because reading theory can be dry and confusing.

In: mask_feature = iris['sepal_length'] > 6.0

In: mask_feature

0False

1False

...

146True

147True

148True

149False

In this example we're trying to select all the lines of our "iris" dataset that have the value of "sepal length" larger than 6. You can clearly see the observations that are either true or false, and therefore know the ones that fit our query. Now let's use a mask in order to change our "iris-virginica" target with a new label. Type:

In: mask_target = iris['target'] == 'Iris-virginica'

In: iris.loc[mask_target, 'target'] = 'New label'

All "Iris-virginica" labels will now be shown as "New label" instead. We are using the "loc()" method to access this data with row and column indexes. Next, let's take a look at the new label list in the "target" column. Type:

In: iris['target'].unique()

Out: array(['Iris-setosa', 'Iris-versicolor', 'New label'], dtype=object)

In this example we are using the "unique" method to examine the new list. Next we can check the statistics by grouping every column. Let's see this in action first, and then discuss how it works. Type:

In: grouped_targets_mean = iris.groupby(['target']).mean()

grouped_targets_mean

Out:

In: grouped_targets_var = iris.groupby(['target']).var()

grouped_targets_var

Out:

We start by grouping each column with the "groupby" method. If you are a bit familiar with SQL, it's worth noting that this works similarly to the "GROUP BY" instruction. Next, we use the "mean" method, which computes the average of the values. This is an aggregate method that can be applied to one or several columns. Then we can have several other pandas methods such as "var" which stands for the variance, "sum" for the summation, "count" for the number of rows, and more. Keep in mind that the result you are looking at is still a data frame. That means that you can link as many operations as you want. In our example we are using the "groupby" method to group the observations by label and then check what the difference is between the values and variances for each of our groups.

Now let's assume the dataset contains a time series. What's a time series, you ask? In data science, sometimes we have to analyze a series of data points that are graphed in a certain chronological order. In other words, it is a sequence of the equally spaced points in time. Time series are used often in statistics, for weather forecasting, and for counting sunspots. Often, these datasets have really noisy data points, so we have to use a "rolling" operation, like this:

In: smooth_time_series = pd.rolling_mean(time_series, 5)

As you can see, we're using the "mean" method again in order to obtain the average of values. You can also replace this method with "median" instead in order to get the median of values. In this example, we also specified that we want to obtain 5 samples.

Now let's explore pandas "apply" method that has many uses due to its ability to perform programmatically operations on rows and columns. Let's see this in action by counting the number of non-zero elements that exist in each line.

In: iris.apply(np.count_nonzero, axis=1).head()

Out:05

15

25

35

45

dtype: int64

Lastly, let's use the "applymap" method for element level operations. In the next example, we are going to assume we want the length of the string representation of each cell. Type:

In: iris.applymap(lambda el:len(str(el))).head()

To receive our value, we need to cast every individual cell to a string value. Once that is done, we can gain the value of the length.

Data Selection with pandas

The final section about working with pandas is data selection. Let's say you find yourself in a situation where your dataset has an index column, and you need to import it and then manipulate it. To visualize this, let's say we have a dataset with an index from 100. Here's how it would look:

n,val1,val2,val3

100,10,10,C

101,10,20,C

102,10,30,B

103,10,40,B

104,10,50,A

So the index of row 0 is 100. If you import such a file, you will have an index column like in our case labeled as "n". There's nothing really wrong with it, however you might use the index column by mistake, so you should separate it instead in order to prevent such errors from happening. To avoid possible issues and errors, all you need to do is mention that "n" is an index column. Here's how to do it:

In: dataset = pd.read_csv('a_selection_example_1.csv', index_col=0) dataset

Out:

Your index column should now be separate. Now let's access the value inside any cell. There's more than one way to do that. You can simply target it by mentioning the column and line. Let's assume we want to obtain "Val3" from the 5th line, which is marked by an index of 104.

In: dataset['val3'][104]

Out: 'A'

Keep in mind that this isn't a matrix, even though it might look like one. Make sure to specify the column first, and then the row in order to extract the value from the cell you want.

Categorical and Numerical Data

Now that we've gone through some basics with pandas, let's learn how to work with the most common types of data, which are numerical and categorical.

Numerical data is quite self-explanatory, as it deals with any data expressed in numbers, such as temperature or sums of money. These numbers can either be integers or floats that are defined with operators such as greater or less than.

Categorical data, on the other hand, is expressed by a value that can't be measured. A great example of this type of data, which is sometimes referred to as nominal data, is the weather, which holds values such as sunny, partially cloudy, and so on. Basically, data to which you cannot apply equal to, greater than, or less than operators is nominal data. Other examples of this data include products you purchase from an online store, computer IDs, IP addresses, etc. Booleans are the one thing that is needed to work with both categorical and numerical data. They can even be used to encode categorical values as numerical values. Let's see an example:

Categorical_feature = sunnynumerical_features = [1, 0, 0, 0, 0]

Categorical_feature = foggynumerical _features = [0, 1, 0, 0, 0]

Categorical_feature = snowynumerical _features = [0, 0, 1, 0, 0]

Categorical_feature = rainynumerical _features = [0, 0, 0, 1, 0]

Categorical_feature = cloudynumerical _features = [0, 0, 0, 0, 1]

Here we take our earlier weather example that takes the categorical data which is in the form of sunny, foggy, etc, and encode them to numerical data. This turns the information into a map with 5 true or false statements for each categorical feature we listed. One of the numerical features (1) confirms the categorical feature, while the other four are o. Now let's turn this result into a dataframe that presents each categorical feature as a column and the numerical features next to that column. To achieve this you need to type the following code:

In: import pandas as pd

```
categorical_feature = pd.Series(['sunny', 'foggy',
'snowy', 'rainy', 'cloudy'])
mapping = pd.get_dummies(categorical_feature)
mapping
```
Out:

In data science, this is called binarization. We do not use one categorical feature with as many levels as we have. Instead, we create all the categorical features and assign two binary values to them. Next we can map the categorical values to a list of numerical values. This is how it would look:

In: mapping['sunny']

Out:

01.0

10.0

20.0

30.0

40.0

Name: sunny, dtype: float64

In: mapping['foggy']

Out:

00.0

11.0

20.0

30.0

40.0

Name: cloudy, dtype: float64

You can see in this example that the categorical value "sunny" is mapped to the following list of Booleans: 1, 0, 0, 0, 0 and you can go on like this for all the other values.

Next up, let's discuss scraping the web for data.

Scraping the Web

You won't always work with already established data sets. So far in our examples, we assumed we already had the data we needed and worked with it as it was. Often, you will have to scrape various web pages to get what you're after and download it. Here are a few real world situations where you will find the need to scrape the web:

1.In finance, many companies and institutions need to scrape the web in order to obtain up to date information about all the organizations in their portfolio. They perform this process on websites belonging to newspaper agencies, social networks, various blogs, and other corporations.

2.Did you use a product comparison website lately to find out where to get the best deal? Well, those websites need to constantly scrape the web in order to update the situation on the market's prices, products, and services.

3.How do advertising companies figure out whether something is popular among people? How do they quantify the feelings and emotions involved with a particular product, service, or even political debate? They scrape the web and analyze the data they find in order to understand people's responses. This enables them to predict how the majority of consumers will respond under similar circumstances.

As you can see, web scraping is necessary when working with data, however working directly with web pages can be difficult because of the different people, server locations, and languages that are involved in creating websites. However, data scientists can rejoice because all websites have one thing in common, and that is HTML. For this reason, web scraping tools focus almost exclusively on working with HTML pages. The most popular tool that is used in data science for this purpose is called Beautiful Soup, and it is written in Python.

Using a tool like Beautiful Soup comes with many advantages. Firstly it enables you to quickly understand and navigate HTML pages. Secondly, it can detect errors and even fill in gaps found in the HTML code of the website. Web designers and developers are humans, after all, and they make mistakes when creating web pages. Sometimes those mistakes can turn into noisy or incomplete data, however Beautiful Soup can rectify this problem.

Keep in mind that Beautiful Soup isn't a crawler that goes through websites to index and copy all their web pages. You simply need to import and use the "urllib" library to download the code behind a webpage, and later import Beautiful Soup to read the data and run it through a parser. Let's first start by downloading a web page.

```
In: import urllib.request
url = 'https://en.wikipedia.org/wiki/Marco_Polo'
request = urllib.request.Request(url)
response = urllib.request.urlopen(request)
```

With this request, we download the code behind Wikipedia's Marco Polo web page. Next up, we use Beautiful Soup to read and parse the resources through its HTML parser.

In: from bs4 import BeautifulSoup

soup = BeautifulSoup(response, 'html.parser')

Now let's extract the web page's title like so:

In: soup.title

Out: <title>Marco Polo - Wikipedia, the free encyclopedia</title>

As you can see, we extracted the HTML title tag, which we can use further for investigation. Let's say you want to know which categories are linked to the wiki page about Marco Polo. You would need to first analyze the page to learn which HTML tag contains the information we want. There is no automatic way of doing this because web information, especially on Wikipedia, constantly changes. You have to analyze the HTML page manually to learn in which section of the page the categories are stored. How do you achieve that? Simply navigate to the Marco Polo webpage, press the F12 key to bring up the web inspector, and go through the code manually. For our example, we find the categories inside a div tag called "mw-normal-catlinks". Here's the code required to print each category and how the output would look:

In:

```
section = soup.find_all(id='mw-normal-catlinks')[0]
for catlink in section.find_all("a")[1:]:
print(catlink.get("title"), "->", catlink.get("href"))
```

Out:

Category:Marco Polo -> /wiki/Category:Marco_Polo

Category:1254 births -> /wiki/Category:1254_births

Category:1324 deaths -> /wiki/Category:1324_deaths

Category:13th-century explorers -> /wiki/Category:13thcentury_explorers

Category: 13th-century venetian people ->/wiki/Category:13thcentury_venetian_people

Category:13th-century venetian writers->/wiki/Category: 13thcentury_venetian_writers

Category:14th-century Italian writers->/wiki/Category: 14thcentury_Italian_writers

In this example, we use the "find all" method to find the HTML text contained in the argument. The method is used twice because we first need to find an ID, and secondly we need to find the "a" tags.

A word of warning when it comes to web scraping- be careful, because it is not always permitted to perform scraping. You might need authorization, because to some websites this minor invasion seems similar to a DoS attack. This confusion can lead the website to ban your IP address. So if you download data this way, read the website's terms and conditions section, or simply contact the moderators to gain more information. Whatever you do, do not try to extract information that is copyrighted. You might find yourself in legal trouble with the website / company owners.

With that being said, let's put pandas away, and look at data processing by using NumPy.

NumPy and Data Processing

Now that you know the basics of loading and preprocessing data with the help of pandas, we can move on to data processing with NumPy. The purpose of this stage is to have a data matrix ready for the next stage, which involves supervised and unsupervised machine learning mechanisms. NumPy data structure comes in the form of ndarray objects, and this is what you will later feed into the machine learning process.

For now, we will start by creating such an object to better understand this phase.

The n-dimensional Array

As it was discussed about Python fundamental data types, lists and dictionaries are some of Python's most important structures. You can build complex data structures with them because they are powerful at storing data, however they're not great at operating on that data. They aren't optimal when it comes to processing power and speed, which are critical when working with complex algorithms. This is why we're using NumPy and its ndarray object, which stands for an "n-dimensional array". Let's look at the properties of a NumPy array:

- It is optimal and fast at transferring data. When you work with complex data, you want the memory to handle it efficiently instead of being bottlenecked.

- You can perform vectorization. In other words, you can make linear algebra computations and specific element operations without being forced to use "for" loops. This is a large plus for NumPy because Python "for" loops cost a lot of resources, making it really expensive to work with a large number of loops instead of ndarrays.

- In data science operations you will have to use tools, or libraries, such as SciPy and Scikit-learn. You can't use them without arrays because they are required as an input, otherwise functions won't perform as intended.

With that being said, here's a few methods of creating a ndarray:

1.    Take an already existing data structure and turn into an array.

2.    Build the array from the start and add in the values later.

3.    You can also upload data to an array even when it's stored on a disk.

Converting a list to a one-dimensional array is a fairly common operation in data science processes. Keep in mind that you have to take into account the type of objects such a list contains. This will have an impact on the dimensionality of the result. Here's an example of this with a list that contains only integers:

In: import numpy as np

int_list = [1,2,3]

```
Array_1 = np.array(int_list)
```

In: Array_1

Out: array([1, 2, 3])

You can access the array just like you access a list in Python. You simply use indexing, and just like in Python, it starts from 0. This is how this operation would look:

In: Array_1[1]

Out: 2

Now you can gain more data about the objects inside the array like so:

In: type(Array_1)

Out: numpy.ndarray

In: Array_1.dtype

Out: dtype('int64')

The result of the dtype is related to the type of operating system you're running. In this example, we're using a 64 bit operating system.

At the end of this exercise, our basic list is transformed into a uni-dimensional array. But what happens if we have a list that contains more than just one type of element? Let's say we have integers, strings, and floats. Let's see an example of this:

In: import numpy as np

```
composite_list = [1,2,3] + [1.,2.,3.] + ['a','b','c']
Array_2 = np.array(composite_list[:3])#here we have
only integers
print ('composite_list[:3]', Array_2.dtype)
Array_2 = np.array(composite _list[:6]) #now we have
integers and floats
print (' composite _list[:6]', Array_2.dtype)
Array_2 = np.array(composite _list) #strings have been
added to the array
print (' composite _list[:] ',Array_2.dtype)
```

Out:

composite _list[:3] int64

composite _list[:6] float64

composite _list[:]  <U32

As you can see, we have a "composite_list" that contains integers, floats, and strings. It's important to understand that when we make an array, we can have any kind of data types and mix them however we wish.

Next, let's see how we can load an array from a file. N-dimensional arrays can be created from the data contained inside a file. Here's an example in code:

```
In: import numpy as np
cars = np.loadtxt('regression-datasets
```

cars.csv',delimiter=',', dtype=float)

In this example, we tell our tool to create an array from a file with the help of the "loadtxt" method by giving it a filename, delimiter, and a data type. It's important to pay attention to the data type (dtype) because if we request a float, but the file contains a string instead, we will receive an error that tells us we cannot convert the string to a float.

Interacting with pandas

Pandas is built on NumPy and they are meant to be used together. This makes it extremely easy to extract arrays from the data frames. Once these arrays are extracted, they can be turned into data frames themselves. Let's take a look at an example:

In: import pandas as pd

import numpy as np

marketing_filename = 'regression-datasets-marketing.csv'

marketing = pd.read_csv(marketing _filename, header=None)

In this phase we are uploading data to a data frame. Next, we're going to use the "values" method in order to extract an array that is of the same type as those contained inside the data frame.

In: marketing _array = marketing.values

marketing _array.dtype

Out: dtype('float64')

We can see that we have a float type array. You can anticipate the type of the array by first using the "dtype" method. This will establish which types are being used by the specified data frame object. Do this before extracting the array. This is how this operation would look:

In: marketing.dtypes

Out:  0float64

1 int64

2float64

3 int64

4float64

5float64

6float64

7float64

8int64

9int64

10int64

11float64

12float64

13float64

dtype: object

Matrix Operations

As a data scientist, you will often have to perform multiplication on two dimensional arrays. This includes matrix calculations, such as matrix to matrix multiplication. Let's create a two dimensional array.

This is a two dimensional array of numbers from 0 to 24. Next, we will declare a vector of coefficients and a column that will stack the vector and its reverse. Here's what it would look like:

Now we can perform the multiplication. Here's an example of multiplying the array with the vector:

In: np.dot(M,coefs)

Out: array([5.,20.,35.,50.,65.])

Here's an example of multiplication between the array and the coefficient vectors:

In: np.dot(M,coefs_matrix)

Out:array([[5.,7.],

[20.,22.],

[35.,37.],

[50.,52.],

[65.,67.]])

In both of these multiplication operations, we used the "np.dot" function in order to achieve them. Next up, let's discuss slicing and indexing.

Slicing and Indexing

Indexing is great for viewing the ndarray by sending an instruction to visualize the slice of columns and rows or the index.

Let's start by creating a 10x10 array. It will initially be two-dimensional.

Next let's extract the rows from 2 to 8, but only the ones that are evenly numbered.

In: M[2:9:2,:]

Out:array([[20, 21, 22, 23, 24, 25, 26, 27, 28, 29],

[40, 41, 42, 43, 44, 45, 46, 47, 48, 49],

[60, 61, 62, 63, 64, 65, 66, 67, 68, 69],

[80, 81, 82, 83, 84, 85, 86, 87, 88, 89]])

Now let's extract the column, but only the ones from index 5.

In: M[2:9:2,5:]

Out:array([[25, 26, 27, 28, 29],

[45, 46, 47, 48, 49],

[65, 66, 67, 68, 69],

[85, 86, 87, 88, 89]])

We successfully sliced the rows and the columns. But what happens if we try a negative index? Doing so would reverse the array. Here's how our previous array would look when using a negative index.

In: M[2:9:2,5::-1]

Out:array([[25, 24, 23, 22, 21, 20],

[45, 44, 43, 42, 41, 40],

[65, 64, 63, 62, 61, 60],

[85, 84, 83, 82, 81, 80]])

There are other ways of slicing and indexing the arrays, but for the purposes of this book it's enough to know how to perform the previously mentioned steps. However, keep in mind that this process is only a way of viewing the data. If you want to use these views further by creating new data, you cannot make any modifications in the original arrays. If you do, it can lead to some negative side effects. In that case, you want to use the "copy" method. This will create a copy of the array which you can modify however you wish. Here's the code line for the copy method:

In: N = M[2:9:2,5:].copy()

Array Stacking

Sometimes, when you work with two dimensional arrays, you may want to add new rows or columns to represent new data and variables. This operation is known as array stacking, and it doesn't take long for NumPy to render the new information. Start by creating a new array:

In: import numpy as np

dataset = np.arange(50).reshape(10,5)

Next, add a new row, and several lines that will be concatenated:

In: single_line = np.arange(1*5).reshape(1,5)

several_lines = np.arange(3*5).reshape(3,5)

Now let's use the vstack method, which stands for vertical stack, to add a new single line.

In: np.vstack((dataset,single_line))

This command line will also work if we want to add several lines.

In: np.vstack((dataset,several_lines))

Next, let's see how to add a variable to the array. This is done with the "hstack" method, which stands for horizontal stack. Here's an example:

In: bias = np.ones(10).reshape(10,1)

np.hstack((dataset,bias))

In this line of code, we added a bias of unit values to the array we created earlier.

As an aspiring data scientist, you will only need to know how to add new rows and columns to your arrays. In most projects you won't need to do more than that, so practice working with two dimensional arrays and NumPy, because this tool is engraved in data science.

# Chapter 3:

# basic linear algebra with exercises

Let's begin with a few basic definitions. You can do algebra without knowing what these words

mean, but this vocabulary is quite useful for discussing how to solve equations. For example, if

your teacher tells you to divide both sides of an equation by the coefficient of x, you won't

understand what to do unless you know what a coefficient is.

• The terms of an equation are separated by + and − signs. For example, there are 4

terms in the equation $5x − 3 = 9 + 2x$. These include the $5x$, the 3, the 9, and the $2x$.

• A variable is an unknown that is represented by a symbol, such as x. For example, there are 2 variables in the equation $3x - 2 + 4y = 3x + 6$. These are x and y.

- A constant is a number that is not a variable. For example, the 3 is a constant in the

equation $y - 3 = x$.

- A constant that multiplies a variable is called a coefficient. For example, there are 2

coefficients in the equation $3x - 4 = 2x$. The coefficients are the 3 and the 2.

- An equation is linear if it consists only of constant terms and terms that are linearly

proportional to the variables; if any variable is raised to a power, like x4, the equation is

not linear. As examples, $4x - 2 = 3$ is a linear equation, while $5x3 - 7x = 9$ is not.

The exercises consist of linear equations with a single variable. The coefficients and other constants are all integers. Now we will discuss some fundamental concepts. It is important to grasp these concepts in order to understand what you

are doing – in addition to being able to do it. We will also describe how to apply these concepts

to solve such linear equations.

The left sides and right sides of an equation are equal. For example, $3 = 1 + 2$ expresses

that 3 is the same as 1 plus 2. Similarly, $4 x = 8 + 2 x$ means that – whatever x is – if you add 8 to

2 times x, it will be equal to 4 times x.

For example, in the equation $2 x + 3 = 9$, you could subtract 3 from both sides,

obtaining $2 x = 9 - 3$, to find that $2 x = 6$. Similarly, you could divide both sides of $2 x = 6$ by 2 to

see that $x = 3$. As a check, $(3) 2 + 3 = 6 + 3 = 9$, so we see that $x = 3$ solves the equation.

**Improve Your Math Fluency Series**

There are a couple of simple rules for what to do to

both sides of a linear equation in order to solve for the variable. The main principle can be summarized in three words: Isolate the unknown. This means to first move all of the unknowns to one side of the equation and all of the constant terms to the other, to collect all of the unknowns in a single term, and then to divide by the coefficient of the unknown.

For example, in $x + 2 = 8$, the 2 is

positive, so subtract 2 from both sides to obtain $x = 8 - 2$. However, in $x - 4 = 6$, the 4 is

negative, so add 4 to both sides to obtain $x = 6 + 4$.

• If there are any variables on the wrong side, move them over with the same technique.

For example, in the equation $3x = 4 + 2x$, the $2x$ is positive, so we subtract $2x$ from

both sides, obtaining $3x - 2x = 4$. In comparison, in $x = 12 - 3x$, the $3x$ is negative, so

we add $3x$ to both sides to get $x + 3x = 12$.

• Once all of the unknowns are on one side and all of the constant terms are on the other,

collect the terms together. For example, the equation 5 x + 3 x − 2 x = 7 − 4 + 3

simplifies to 6 x = 6 (since 5 + 3 − 2 = 6 and 7 − 4 + 3 = 6).

• Now divide both sides of the equation by the coefficient of the unknown. For example,

if 4 x = 24, divide both sides by 4 to find that x = 24 / 4 = 6.

• If your answer is a fraction, check to see if it can be reduced. For example, 6/9 can be

reduced to 2/3.

For 6/9, the greatest common factor is 3 because 6 = (3) (2) and 9 = (3)(3). That is, both the 6 and 9 have the 3 in common as a factor. For 12/24, the greatest common factor is 12 since 24 = (12) (2).

For 12/24, dividing 12 and 24 both by 12 results in 1/2. Therefore, 12/24 = 1/2.

# Chapter 4:
# Statistics and basic concept

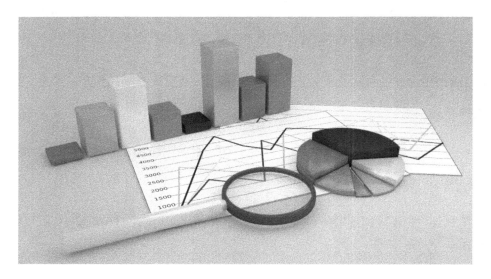

We live in an age and society where we trust technology and quantifiable information more than we trust each other—and sometimes ourselves.

The gut feeling and great conviction of Steve Jobs to know "what consumers would later want" is revered and romanticized. And yet there's sparse business literature (Blink by Malcolm Gladwell is a notable exception), an eerie absence of online learning courses, and little sign of a mainstream movement promoting one person's unaided intuition as the key to commercial success.

Everyone is too preoccupied; we're busy thinking about quantitative evidence and especially the personal data generated by Apple's expanding suite of products. Extensive customer profiling and procuring data designed to wrench out our every inner desire are dominant and pervasive trends in business today.

Perhaps Jobs represents a statistical anomaly. His legacy cannot be wiped from the dataset, but few in the business world would set out to emulate him without data in their pocket. As Wired Magazine's Editor-in-chief Chris Anderson extols, we don't need theories but rather data to look at and analyze in this age of big data.

Data—both big and small—is collected constantly: how far we travel each day, who we interact with on the web and where we spend our money. Every bit of data has a story to tell. But, left isolated, these parcels of information rest dormant and underutilized—equivalent to Lego blocks cordoned into bags of separate pieces.

However, like Lego laid out neatly across the floor, data is extraordinarily versatile in the hands of the right operator. It can be merged and arranged to serve in a variety of ways and rearranged to derive value beyond its primary purpose. A parade of data's secondary value was orchestrated in 2002 when Amazon made a deal with AOL to access and manage their e-commerce platform. Importantly, the agreement granted Amazon access to the e-commerce platform's user data. While AOL viewed their data in terms of its primary value (recorded sales data), Amazon saw a secondary value that would improve its proficiency to push personalized product recommendations to users. By gaining access to data that documented what AOL users were browsing and purchasing, Amazon's main aim was to improve the performance of its own product recommendation engine, explains Amazon's former Chief Scientist Andreas Weigend.

Various fields of data analytics including machine learning, data mining, and deep learning continue to improve our ability to unlock hidden patterns in data for direct analysis or secondary use as typified by Amazon.

In the 18th Century John Graunt developed the first "life table," which surmised the probability of survival for a range of different age groups during a public health crisis that swept Europe in the mid-1600s. By analyzing the weekly bills of mortality (deaths), Graunt and Petty attempted to create a warning system to offset the spread of the bubonic plague in London. While the system was never implemented, it served as a useful statistical estimation of London's large population at the time.

Probability theory evolved during this same period by way of new theories published by Gerolamo Cardano, Blaise Pascal, and Pierre de Fermat. As an accomplished Italian chess player and gambler, Cardano observed dice games to comprehend and distill the basic concepts of probability. This included the ability to produce a desired result by defining odds as the ratio of favorable to unfavorable outcomes. Although he wrote Liber de ludo aleae (Book on Games of Chance) in 1564, the book wasn't published until a century later in the year 1663. Beyond its section on effective cheating methods, Cardano's thesis was positively received as the first systematic treatment of probability.

A decade earlier, in 1654, the Frenchmen Pierre de Fermat and Blaise Pascal (also known for his work on the arithmetical triangle and co-inventor of the mechanical calculator) collaborated to develop the concept of expected value, which was again developed for the purpose of better understanding gambling outcomes. To end a game early, Pascal and de Fermet devised a method to divide the stakes equitably based on the probability each player had of winning. This study into the mathematical theory of probability helped to develop the concept of expected value or the law of large numbers. Pascal and de Fermat found that as the number of independent trials increases, the average of the outcomes nears toward an expected value, which is calculated as the sum of all possible values multiplied by the probability of its occurrence. For example, if you continually roll a six-sided dice, the expected average value of all the results is close to 3.5.

Example

$(1 + 2 + 3 + 4 + 5 + 6) \times (1/6)$

$21 \times 0.16666666666667$

$= 3.5$

In the 18th Century, advancements in probability theory and the study of demography (based on Graunt's prior work in census studies) combined to spawn the modern field of statistics.

Derived from the Latin stem "sta," meaning "to stand, set down, make or be firm," the field of statistics was initially limited to discussions about policy and the condition of the state. [4] The earliest known recording of the term was the use of the German word "statistik," which was popularized and supposedly coined by the German political scientist Gottfried Aschenwall (1719-1772) in his 1748 publication Vorbereitung zur Staatswissenschaft.[5]

The German word "statistik" is thought to have borrowed from the Modern Latin term "statisticum collegium" (lecture course on state affairs), the Italian word "statista" (statesman or one skilled in statecraft), and the Latin word "status" (meaning a station, position, place, order, arrangement, or condition).[6] The new term was later published in the English-speaking world by Sir John Sinclair in his 1791 publication the Statistical Account of Scotland.

By the late 18th Century, the term "statistics" had become synonymous with the systematic collection and analysis of a state's demographic and economic information. The regular recording of state resources had been in practice since ancient times, but deeper than an exercise in state bookkeeping, the new moniker inspired specialist studies into using data to inform decision-making and incorporated the latest methods in probability and data distribution.

Statistics later expanded in scope during the 19th Century. No longer confined to assessing the condition of the state, attention was recalibrated to all fields of study, including medicine and sport, which is how we recognize statistics today.

But while emerging fields like "machine learning" and "data mining" sound new and exciting, "statistics" tends to evoke memories of a dry and compulsory class taught in high school or college. In the book Naked Statistics: Stripping the Dread from the Data, author Charles Wheelan writes that students often complain that "statistics is confusing and irrelevant," but outside the classroom, they are to glad discuss batting averages, the wind chill factor, grade point averages and how to reliably measure the performance of an NFL quarterback.[7] As Wheelan observes, most people learn statistics at some stage in their life, but few people know how to apply these advanced theories past examination day despite an inherent curiosity and interest in measuring things—especially performance.

This dichotomy, though, is beginning to change with the recent popularity of data science, which has grown in favor since Charles Wheelan's book was published in 2012. From the planning of data collection to advanced techniques of analysis, statistics is applied across nearly all corners of data science. Machine learning, in particular, has substantial overlap with inferential statistics, which entails extracting a sample from a pool of data and making generalized predictions about the full population. Like inferential statistics, machine learning draws on a set of observations to discover underlying patterns that can then be used to form predictions.

In this absolute beginners' introduction to statistics, we focus primarily on inferential statistics to prepare you for further study in the field of data science or other areas of quantitative research where statistical inference is applied. This includes an introduction to essential techniques used to infer predictions from data, such as hypothesis testing, linear regression analysis, confidence levels, probability theory, and data distribution. Descriptive statistical methods such as central tendency measures and standard deviation are introduced as well in this title.

As a branch of mathematics, statistics involves studying how data is collected, organized, analyzed, interpreted, and presented. The goal of statistics is to determine the meaning of the data and whether variations, if any, are meaningful or due merely to chance.

The alternative to statistical analysis is aptly named non-statistical analysis and is a form of qualitative analysis. Non-statistical analysis collects non-quantitative information gathered from text, sound, and moving and still images to inform decision-making. This form of analysis, however, is far less scalable and practical for analyzing large trends and patterns.

Descriptive vs Inferential Statistics

Quantitative analysis can be split into two major branches of statistics: descriptive statistics and inferential statistics. Descriptive statistics helps to organize data and provides a summary of data features numerically and/or graphically. Typical methods of descriptive statistics include the mode (most common value), mean (average value), standard deviation (variance), and quartiles.

As a critical distinction from inferential statistics, descriptive statistics applies to scenarios where all values in the dataset are known. In the case of an e-commerce website, this would mean access to information about all the registered users of the platform and then using descriptive statistics to summarize that information including total average spending (mean), the most common bracket of spending (mode) or the variance in customer spending activity (standard deviation). With a complete dataset, the findings should accurately summarize and reflect the characteristics and patterns of the defined population.

Sport is an example of a field that draws heavily on descriptive statistics to generate individual player and team metrics, such as batting averages, assists, and points per game as each event is reliably logged and recorded.

In the case of inferential statistics, there's no longer the luxury of a full population. The analysis is instead subject to the nuances of probability theory, dealing with random phenomena and inferring what is likely and what is unlikely.

When a full census is not possible or feasible, a selected subset, called a sample, is extracted from the population. "Population" refers to an entire group of items, such as people, animals, transactions, or purchases. The selection of the sample data from the population is naturally subject to an element of randomness. Inferential statistics is then applied to develop models to extrapolate the study's findings from the sample data to draw inferences about the entire population while accounting for the influence of randomness.

To better explain how inferential statistics works, let's consider a large online platform like YouTube, which as of 2017, entertains 1.5 billion logged in users each month. [8] Rather than scrutinize the entire population of monthly logged in users, we can create a sample dataset of 10,000 users that can be analyzed to form predictions about the full population of YouTube users.

Naturally, the 10,000 users we select won't precisely represent 1.5 billion people. Although we can attempt to collect a sample dataset representative of the full population, some margin of error is inevitable and, in fact, expected. In inferential statistics, we account for this discrepancy or margin of error with what is known as confidence, which is a statistical measure of prediction confidence.

Specifically, confidence is a measure to express how closely the sample results match the true value of the full population. This takes the form of a percentage value between 0% and 100%, which is called the confidence level. The closer the confidence level is to 100%, the more confident we are of the experiment's results. A confidence level of 95%, for example, means that if we repeat the experiment numerous times (under the same conditions), the results will match that of the full population in 95% of all possible cases. Alternatively, a confidence level of 0% expresses that we have no confidence in repeating the results in further experiments.

Note, though, that it's impossible to have a confidence level of 100%. The only way to prove the results are 100% accurate is by analyzing the entire population, which would render the study descriptive rather than inferential.

Hypothesis Testing

A crucial part of inferential statistics is hypothesis testing, in which you evaluate two mutually exclusive statements to determine which statement is correct given the data presented. Due to the absence of a complete dataset, hypothesis testing is applied in inferential statistics to determine whether there's reasonable evidence from the sample data to infer that a particular condition holds true of the full population.

Hypothesis tests are constructed around a hypothesis statement, which is a prediction of a given outcome or assumption. For example, you might propose there to be no direct relationship between a CEO's salary and the number of syllables in their surname. In this example, the (independent) variable you're testing is the number of syllables in the CEO's surname. If you discover that this independent variable does not affect a CEO's salary (the dependent variable), this confirms the null hypothesis. It's important to note that the term "null" doesn't mean "invalid" or associated with the value zero but rather a hypothesis that the researcher attempts or wishes to "nullify."

Let's turn to an example to explain this concept. For most of human history, people thought all swans were white and dark-colored feathers did not exist within the confines of mother nature. The null hypothesis that swans have white feathers was dispelled after Dutch explorers discovered black swans in Western Australia in 1697.

Prior to this discovery, "black swan" was a euphemism for "impossible" or "non-existent," but after this finding, it morphed into a term to express a perceived impossibility that might become an eventuality and therefore disproven. In recent times, the term "black swan" has been popularized by the literary work of Nassim Taleb to explain unforeseen events such as the rise of the Internet, World War I, and the breakup of the Soviet Union.

Next, a hypothesis statement must be clear and simple. A clear hypothesis tests only one relationship and avoids conjunctions such as "and," "nor" and "or." According to California State University Bakersfield, a good hypothesis should include an "if" and "then" statement, such as: If [I study statistics] then [my employment opportunities increase]. The first half of this sentence structure generally contains an independent variable (i.e., study statistics) and a dependent variable in the second half (i.e., employment opportunities). A dependent variable represents what you're attempting to predict, and the independent variable is the variable that supposedly impacts the outcome of the dependent variable.

Hypotheses are also most effective when based on existing knowledge, intuition, or prior research. Hypothesis statements are seldom chosen at random.

Finally, a good hypothesis statement should be testable through an experiment, controlled test or observation. Designing an effective hypothesis test that reliably assesses your assumptions, however, is somewhat complicated and even when implemented correctly can lead to unintended consequences.

Cardiovascular disease, for instance, was a rare ailment up until the second half of the 20th Century. Nutritional scientists began investigating possible causes for its increasing occurrence after it became the leading cause of death in America in the 1950sThese studies linked cardiovascular disease and high cholesterol levels with saturated animal fats contained in butter, meat, cheese, and eggs.

The study was carried out by the famous nutritionist Ancel Keys, who helped research and design the U.S. army's rations during the Second World War. The study found that men from countries that consume large amounts of saturated fats have a higher rate of heart disease than those living in countries that consume mainly grains, fish, nuts, and vegetables. Randomized controlled trials in the 1980's also concluded that saturated fats, including beef tallow, were unhealthy. These events and public protest provoked the fast food giant McDonald's to shelve and modify their famous French fries recipe. More recent studies, though, have found that the proclaimed nutritional alternative to saturated animal fats, vegetable oils, are doing our body greater harm as a result of carboxylic acids.

Each of these studies started with a clear hypothesis, but they generated polarizing outcomes regarding the question of whether we should consume food cooked in animal fats.

# Chapter 5:

# Decision tree and how to use them.

**The Decision Trees**

We now know a bit about how supervised machine learning is going to work. It is time to look at some specific examples of how these learning algorithms are going to work. And the first one we will look at is known as a decision tree learning algorithm.

With this one, you will find a lot of efficiencies when it comes to data, especially if you are taking a look at a few different options and you want to figure out which method is going to be the right decision for your business or on your project. When there are a few options presented with the decision tree, you get the benefit of seeing the possibilities and the outcomes that each one is going to produce for you. This is often one of the most efficient and accurate ways to make sure that the decisions fit your needs.

There are different times when you would want to work with a decision tree. You may find working with it for a continuous random variable or for some of the other categorical variables that are available. However, you will usually use this kind of learning algorithm in order to do classification problems.

To help you make a good decision tree, you need to be able to split up whole domain sets so that you get two sets at least, often three or more, of similar data. These will then be sorted out, using their independent variables, because it is going to help you to distinguish out the different sets that you have in front of you.

This brings up the question of how you will be able to make all of this work. Let's say that we have a group of people, 60 of them. Each person in that group will have three independent variables that will include their gender, height, and class. When you take a look at this ground, you know from the beginning that 30 of these students like to play soccer when they have some free time. You can work with the decision tree in order to figure out which people in that group like to play soccer and which don't.

To help you with this one, you can take the learning algorithm for a decision tree and look at that group of people before dividing them into some groups. You would need to use the variables of height, class, and gender to help with this. The hope with this is that when the whole thing is done, you can end up with a homogenous set of people.

Of course, there are going to be a few others of the learning algorithms that you are able to use in order to do this, and they may work well with the decision tree to help you split up some of the data that you are working with. This is going to give you a minimum of two kinds of subsets that will produce outcomes that are pretty homogenous. Remember that it is possible to have more, but since we just want to know whether the group is going to be soccer players or not, then we just want to work with two groups.

Decision trees are going to be a good option for programmers to choose because they make it really easy to split up all of your data, and then you can make some good decisions based from what shows up in that data. It is a good way to help you make some great decisions for your business because you will be able to get all of your information out in front of you to make decisions, rather than just having to guess.

**Random Forests**

The next type of learning algorithm that you are able to work with is the random forest. There are a lot of times when the decision tree is going to work out well for you, but there are times when you may want to make this a bit different, and the random forest is going to be the right option for you.

One time, when you would want to work with a random forest, is when you would like to work with some task that can take your data and explore it, like dealing with any of the values in the set of data that is missing or if you would like to be able to handle any of the outliers to that data set.

This is one of the times when you are going to want to choose the random forest rather than working with the decision trees, and knowing which time to use each of these different learning algorithms. Some examples of when the programmer would want to work with a random forest include:

- When you are working on your own training sets, you will find that all of the objects that are inside a set will be generated randomly, and it can be replaced if your random tree thinks that this is necessary and better for your needs.

- If there are M input variable amounts, then $m<M$ is going to be specified from the beginning, and it will be held as a constant. The reason that this is so important is that it means that each tree that you have is randomly picked from their own variable using M.

- The goal of each of your random trees will be to find the split that is the best for the variable m.

- As the tree grows, all of these trees are going to keep getting as big as they possibly can. Remember that these random trees are not going to prune themselves.

The forest that is created from a random tree can be great because it is much better at predicting certain outcomes. It is able to do this for you because it will take all prediction from each of the trees that you create, and then will be able to select the average for regression or the consensus that you get during the classification.

These random forests are going to be the tool that you want to use many times with the various parts of data science, and this makes them very advantageous compared to the other options. First, these algorithms are able to handle any kind of problem that you are focusing on, both the regression and classification problems. Most of the other learning algorithms that you will encounter in this guidebook are only able to handle one type of problem rather than all of them.

Another benefit of these random forests is that they are going to help you handle large amounts of data. If your business has a lot of different points that you want to go through and organize, then the random forest is one of the algorithms that you need to at least consider.

There is a limitation that comes with using random forests though, which is why you will not be able to use it with all of the problems that you want to take on. For example, this can work with regression problems like we talked about before, but they are not going to be able to make any kind of prediction that goes past the range that you add to your training data. You will be able to get some predictions, of course, but these predictions will end up becoming limited. It will stop at the ranges that you provide, lowering the amount of accuracy that is found there.

**KNN Algorithm**

Next on the list of learning algorithms that we are going to take a look at is the K-nearest neighbors, or KNN, algorithm. This is one that is used a lot in supervised machine learning, so it is worth our time to take a look at it here. When you work with the KNN algorithm, you are going to use it to help take a lot of data and search through it. The goal is to have k-most similar examples for any data instance that you would like to work with. When you get this all organized in the proper manner, this KNN algorithm will be able to take a look through that set of data, and then it will summarize the results before using these to make the right predictions that you need.

A lot of businesses will use this kind of model in order to help them become more competitive with the kind of learning that they are able to do in the industry. This is going to work because there will be a few elements in this model that will compete against each other. The elements that end up winning in here are going to be the way that you are the most successful and you get the prediction that will work the best for you.

Compared to the other two learning algorithms that are out there, this one is going to be a bit different. In fact, some programmers are going to see this as one of the lazier learning processes because it is not able to really create any models unless you go through and ask it to do a new prediction. This is a good thing for some projects if you would like to keep the information in the models relevant or have more say in what you are adding to the models, but in other situations, it is not going to be all that helpful.

There are a lot of benefits of working with the KNN learning algorithm. For example, when you choose to use this kind of algorithm, you can learn how to cut out the noise that sometimes shows up inside the set of data. The reason that this works is that it is going to work solely with the method of competition to help sort through all of the data in the hopes of finding the stuff that is the most desirable. This algorithm is useful because it can take in a lot of data, even larger amounts, at the same time which can be useful in a lot of different situations.

However, you are going to run into a few conditions to consider when it comes to this algorithm. The biggest issue is that there are high amounts of costs computationally, especially when you compare it to what some of the other learning algorithms will do. This is because KNN is going to look through the points, all of them before it sends you a prediction. This takes a lot of time and money overall, and may not be the one that you want to use.

## Regression Algorithms

Next on the list is the regression algorithm. You will be able to use this because it is a type where you will investigate the relationship that is there between the dependent variables and the predictor variables that you like to use. You will find that this is the method a programmer will want to work with any time they see there is a casual relationship between the forecasting that you do, the time-series modeling, and all of the variables.

You will want to work with these regression algorithms any time that you want to take all of the different points in your set of data and you want it to fit onto a line or a curve as closely as possible. This helps you to really see if there are some factors that are common between these data points so that you can learn about the data and maybe make some predictions as well.

Many programmers and companies are going to use this kind of regression algorithm in order to help them make great predictions that then help the business to grow, along with their profits. You will be able to use it in order to figure out a good estimation of the growth in sales that the company is looking for, while still being able to base it on how the conditions of the economy in the market are doing now and how they will do in the future.

The neat thing about these kinds of learning algorithms is that you are able to place in any kind of information that seems to be pertinent for your needs. You are able to add in some information about the economy, both how it has acted in the present and in the past so that this learning algorithm is able to figure out what may happen to your business in the future. The information that you add to this needs to be up to date and easy to read through, or this algorithm could run into some issues.

Let's take a look at an example of how this can work. If you go with the regression algorithm and find that your company is growing near or at the same rate that other industries have been doing in this kind of economy, then it is possible to take that new information and use it to make some predictions about how your company will do in the future based on whether the economy goes up or down or even stays the same.

There are going to be more than one option of learning algorithms that you are able to work with when we explore these regression algorithms. And you will have to take a look at some of the benefits and the differences between them all to figure out which one is the right for you. There are a lot of options when it comes to picking out an algorithm that you would like to use, but some of the most common of these will include:

1. Stepwise regression

2. Logistic regression

3. Linear regression

4. Ridge regression

5. Polynomial regression

Any time that you decide to work with one of these learning algorithms, you are going to be able to see quickly whether or not there is a relationship between your dependent and independent variables, as well as what that relationship is all about. This kind of algorithm is going to be there because it shows the company the impact that they have to deal with if they try to add or change the variables in the data. This allows for some experimentation so that you can see what changes are going to work the best for you and which ones don't.

There are going to be a few negatives and shortcomings that you have to work within the regression algorithms. The first one is that you can only use these in regression problems (like the name suggests) and not in any kind of classification problems. This is because this kind of algorithm is going to spend too much time overfitting the data that you have. This makes the process tedious and it is best if you are able to avoid working on it at all.

## Naïve Bayes

And finally, we are going to move on to the other supervised machine learning method that we need to look at. This one is known as the Naïve Bayes method, and it is going to be really useful in a lot of the different kinds of programs that you want to create, especially if you are looking to showcase your model to others, even those who don't understand how all of this is supposed to work.

To help us get a better understanding of how this learning algorithm is going to work, we need to spend some time bringing out our imaginations a bit. For this one, imagine that you are working on some program or problem that needs classification. In this, you want to be able to come up with a new hypothesis to go with it, and then you want to be able to design some new features and discussions that are based on how important the variables in that data are going to be.

Once all of the information is sorted out, and you are ready to work on the model that you want to use and then enter the shareholders. These shareholders want to know what is going on with the model and want to figure out what kinds of predictions and results you are going to be able to get from your needs. This brings up the question, how are you going to be able to show all of the information you are working on to the shareholders before the work is even done? And how you are going to be able to do this in a way that is easier to understand?

The good thing to consider with this one is that the Naïve Bayes algorithm is going to be able to help you, even in the earliest stages of your model, so that you can organize everything and show others what is going on. The learning algorithm is going to be what you will need to use in order to do a demonstration to show off your model, even when it is still found in one of the earlier stages of development.

This may seem a bit confusing right now, but it is time to look at an example to help us explain how to make this happen with some apples. When you go to the store and grab an apple that looks pretty average to you. When you grab this apple, you will be able to go through and state out some of the features that distinguish the apple from some of the other fruits that are out there. Maybe you will say that it is about three inches round, that it is red, and has a stem.

Yes, some of these features are going to be found in other types of fruit, but the fact that all of them show up in the product at the same time means that you have an apple instead of another type of product in your hand. This is a simple way of thinking about an apple and figuring out how it is different from some of the others out there, but it is a good example of what is going to happen when you use the Naïve Bayes algorithm.

A programmer is likely to work with the Naïve Bayes model when they want to have something that is easy to get started with, and when they have a lot of data or a large data set, that they want to be able to simplify a bit. One of the biggest uses of this kind of algorithm is that it is going to be simple to use, and even if you could do things in a more sophisticated method, it is a better option to go with.

As you learn more about the Naïve Bayes algorithm, you will start to see more and more reasons in order to work with it. This kind of model is going to be an easy one to use and it is the most effective when it comes to predicting the class of your test data so that it becomes one of the best choices for anyone who would like to keep the process simple or those who are new to working with the machine learning process for the first time. The neat thing here though is, though this is a simple algorithm to bring up, it is still able to be used in the same way that higher-class algorithms can do.

Of course, just like with some of the other supervised learning algorithms that you would lie to work with, there are going to be some negatives that show up along the way. First, when you need to do some variables that are categorical, and you want to go through and test some data that hasn't been able to go through the set of data for training, you may find that the model is not going to make the best predictions for you and the probability is not going to be the best either.

If you still want to use the Naïve Bayes algorithm even with some of these issues, there are a few methods that you can work with to solve the problem. The Laplace estimation is a good example of this. But the more methods that you add in, the more complication are going to show up and that kind of beats the purpose of working with this. Keeping it simple and knowing when you are able to use this algorithm will help you to get the results that you want.

This is a good method to use, but realize that you will not pull it out all of the time. If you have a lot of information that you would like to work on, and you need to be able to take that information and show it off in a manner that is simple and easy to understand, then this learning algorithm is going to be a good option for you.

These are just a few of the different options that you are able to work with when it comes to working with supervised machine learning. This is one of the easiest types of machine learning that you are able to work with, and it is going to prove to be really useful overall. Try out a few of these learning algorithms and see how supervised machine learning works before we take some time to move on to the other two types as well.

# Chapter 6:

# Languages required for data science.

### *Basics of python*

Keywords are an important part of Python programming; they are words that are reserved for use by Python itself. You can't use these names for anything other than what they are intended for, and you most definitely can't use them as part of an identifier name, such as a function or a variable. Reserved keywords are used for defining the structure and the syntax of Python. There are, at the present time, 33 of these words, and one thing you must remember is that they are case sensitive—only three of them are capitalized, and the rest are in lower case. These are the keywords, written exactly as they appear in the language:

- False

- if

- assert

- as

- is

- global

- in

- pass

- finally

- try

- not

- while

- return

- None

- for

- True

- class

- break

- elif

- continue

- yield

- and

- del

- with

- import

- else

- def

- except

- from

- or

- lambda

- nonlocal

- raise

Note: only True, False, and None are capitalized.

The identifiers are the names that we give to things like variables, functions, classes, etc., and the name is just so that we can identify one from another. There are certain rules that you must abide by when you write an identifier:

• You may use a combination of lowercase letters (a to z), uppercase letters (A to Z), digits (0 to 9), and the underscore (_). Names such as func_2, myVar and print_to_screen are all examples of perfectly valid identifier names.

• You may not start an identifier name with a digit, so 2Class would be invalid, whereas class2 is valid.

• You may not, as mentioned above, use a reserved keyword in the identifier name. For example:

```
>>> global = 2
  File "<interactive input>", line 3
    global = 2
         ^
```

Would give you an error message of:

SyntaxError: invalid syntax

- You may not use any special symbols, such as $, %, #, !, etc., in the identifier name. For example:

>>> a$ = 1

  File "<interactive input>", line 13

    A$ = 1

    ^

Would also give you the following error message:

SyntaxError: invalid syntax

An identifier name can be any length you require.

Things to note are:

- Because the Python programming language is case sensitive, variable and Variable would mean different things.

- Make sure your identifier names reflect what the identifier does. For example, while you could get away with writing c = 12, it would make more sense to write count = 12. You know at a glance exactly what it does, even if you don't look at the code for several weeks.

- Use underscores where possible to separate a name made up of multiple words, for example, this_variabe_has_ many_words

You may also use camel case. This is a writing style where the first letter of every word is capitalized except for the first one, for example, thisVariableHasManyWords.

of time.

### *Advantages of Machine Learning*

Due to the sheer volume and magnitude of the tasks, there are some instances where an engineer or developer cannot succeed, no matter how hard they try; in those cases, the advantages of machines over humans are clearly stark.

Identifies Patterns

When the engineer feeds a machine with artificial intelligence a training data set, it will then learn how to identify patterns within the data and produce results for any other similar inputs that the engineer provides the machine with. This is efficiency far beyond that of a normal analyst. Due to the strong connection between machine learning and data science (which is the process of crunching large volumes of data and unearthing relationships between the underlying variables), through machine learning, one can derive important insights into large volumes of data.

Improves Efficiency

Humans might have designed certain machines without a complete appreciation for their capabilities, since they may be unaware of the different situations in which a computer or machine will work. Through machine learning and artificial intelligence, a machine will learn to adapt to environmental changes and improve its own efficiency, regardless of its surroundings.

Completes Specific Tasks

A programmer will usually develop a machine to complete certain tasks, most of which involving an elaborate and arduous program where there is scope for the programmer to make errors of omission. He or she might forget about a few steps or details that they should have included in the program. An artificially intelligent machine that can learn on its own would not face these challenges, as it would learn the tasks and processes on its own.

## Helps Machines Adapt to the Changing Environment

With ever-changing technology and the development of new programming languages to communicate these technological advancements, it is nearly impossible to convert all existing programs and systems into these new syntaxes. Redesigning every program from its coding stage to adapt to technological advancements is counterproductive. At such times, it is highly efficient to use machine learning so that they can upgrade and adapt to the changing technological climate all on their own.

## Helps Machines Handle Large Data Sets

Machine learning brings with it the capability to handle multiple dimensions and varieties of data simultaneously and in uncertain conditions. An artificially intelligent machine with abilities to learn on its own can function in dynamic environments, emphasizing the efficient use of resources.

Machine learning has helped to develop tools that provide continuous improvements in quality in small and larger process environments.

Disadvantages of Machine Learning

•      It is difficult to acquire data to train the machine. The engineer must know what algorithm he or she wants to use to train it, and only then can he or she identify the data set they will need to use to do so. There can be a significant impact on the results obtained if the engineer does not make the right decision.

•      It's difficult to interpret the results accurately to determine the effectiveness of the machine-learning algorithm.

•      The engineer must experiment with different algorithms before he or she chooses one to train the machine with.

•      Technology that surpasses machine learning is being researched; therefore, it is important for machines to constantly learn and transform to adapt to new technology.

## Subjects Involved in Machine Learning

Machine learning is a process that uses concepts from multiple subjects. Each of these subjects helps a programmer develop a new method that can be used in machine learning, and all these concepts together form the discipline of the topic. This section covers some of the subjects and languages that are used in machine learning.

## Statistics

A common problem in statistics is testing a hypothesis and identifying the probability distribution that the data follows. This allows the statistician to predict the parameters for an unknown data set. Hypothesis testing is one of the many concepts of statistics that are used in machine learning. Another concept of statistics that's used in machine learning is predicting the value of a function using its sample values. The solutions to such problems are instances of machine learning, since the problems in question use historical (past) data to predict future events. Statistics is a crucial part of machine learning.

## Brain Modeling

Neural networks, are closely related to machine learning. Scientists have suggested that nonlinear elements with weighted inputs can be used to create a neural network. Extensive studies are being conducted to assess these elements.

## Adaptive Control Theory

Adaptive control theory is a part of this subject that deals with methods that help the system adapt to such changes and continue to perform optimally. The idea is that a system should anticipate the changes and modify itself accordingly.

## Psychological Modeling

For years, psychologists have tried to understand human learning. The EPAM network is a method that's commonly used to understand human learning. This network is utilized to store and retrieve words from a database when the machine is provided with a function. The concepts of semantic networks and decision trees were only introduced later. In recent times, research in psychology has been influenced by artificial intelligence.

Another aspect of psychology called reinforcement learning has been extensively studied in recent times, and this concept is also used in machine learning.

## Artificial Intelligence

As mentioned earlier, a large part of machine learning is concerned with the subject of artificial intelligence. Studies in artificial intelligence have focused on the use of analogies for learning purposes and on how past experiences can help in anticipating and accommodating future events. In recent years, studies have focused on devising rules for systems that use the concepts of inductive logic programming and decision tree methods.

## Evolutionary Models

A common theory in evolution is that animals prefer to learn how to better adapt to their surroundings to enhance their performance. For example, early humans started to use the bow and arrow to protect themselves from predators that were faster and stronger than them. As far as machines are concerned, the concepts of learning and evolution can be synonymous with each other. Therefore, models used to explain evolution can also be utilized to devise machine learning techniques. The most prominent technique that has been developed using evolutionary models is the genetic algorithm.

Programming Languages

R

R is a programming language that is estimated to have close to 2 million users. This language has grown rapidly to become very popular since its inception in 1990. It is a common belief that R is not only a programming language for statistical analysis but can also be used for multiple functions. This tool is not limited to only the statistical domain. There are many features that make it a powerful language.

The programming language R is one that can be used for many purposes, especially by data scientists to analyze and predict information through data. The idea behind developing R was to make statistical analysis easier.

As time passed, the language began to be used in different domains. There are many people who are adept at coding in R, although they are not statisticians. This situation has arisen since many packages are being developed that help to perform functions like data processing, graphic visualization, and other analyses. R is now used in the spheres of finance, genetics, language processing, biology, and market research.

Python

Python is a language that has multiple paradigms. You can probably think of Python as a Swiss Army knife in the world of coding, since this language supports structured programming, object-oriented programming, functional programming, and other types of programming. Python is the second-best language in the world since it can be used to write programs in every industry and for data mining and website construction.

The creator, Guido Van Possum, decided to name the language Python, after Monty Python. If you were to use some inbuilt packages, you would find that there are some sketches of the Monty Python in the code or documentation. It is for this reason and many others that Python is a language that most programmers love, though engineers or those with a scientific background who are now data scientists would find it difficult to work with.

Python's simplicity and readability make it quite easy to understand. The numerous libraries and packages available on the internet demonstrate that data scientists in different sectors have written programs that are tailored to their needs and are available to download.

Since Python can be extended to work best for different programs, data scientists have begun to use it to analyze data. It is best to learn how to code in Python since it will help you analyze and interpret data and identify solutions that will work best for a business.

# Chapter 7:
# Neural network and what to use for?

Regular deep neural networks commonly receive a single vector as an input and then transform it through a series of multiple hidden layers. Every hidden layer in regular deep neural networks, in fact, is made up of a collection of neurons in which every neuron is fully connected to all contained neurons from the previous layers. In addition, all neurons contained in a deep neural network are completely independent as they do not share any relations or connections.

The last fully-connected layer in regular deep neural networks is called the output layer and in every classification setting, this output layer represents the overall class score.

Due to these properties, regular deep neural nets are not capable of scaling to full images. For instance, in CIFAR-10, all images are sized as 32x32x3. This means that all CIFAR-10 images gave 3 color channels and that they are 32 wide and 32 inches high. This means that a single fully-connected neural network in a first regular neural net would have 32x32x3 or 3071 weights. This is an amount that is not manageable as those fully-connected structures are not capable of scaling to larger images.

In addition, you would want to have more similar neurons to quickly add-up more parameters. However, in this case of computer vision and other similar problems, using fully-connected neurons is wasteful as your parameters would lead to over-fitting of your model very quickly. Therefore, convolutional neural networks take advantage of the fact that their inputs consist of images for solving these kinds of deep learning problems.

Due to their structure, convolutional neural networks constrain the architecture of images in a much more sensible way. Unlike a regular deep neural network, the layers contained in the convolutional neural network are comprised of neurons that are arranged in three dimensions including depth, height, and width. For instance, the CIFAR-10 input images are part of the input volume of all layers contained in a deep neural network and the volume comes with the dimensions of 32x32x3.

The neurons in these kinds of layers can be connected to only a small area of the layer before it, instead of all the layers being fully-connected like in regular deep neural networks. In addition, the output of the final layers for CIFAR-10 would come with dimensions of 1x1x10 as the end of convolutional neural networks architecture would have reduced the full image into a vector of class score arranging it just along the depth dimension.

To summarize, unlike the regular-three-layer deep neural networks, a ConvNet composes all its neurons in just three dimensions. In addition, each layer contained in convolutional neural network transforms the 3D input volume into a 3D output volume containing various neuron activations. A convolutional neural network contains layers that all have a simple API resulting in

3D output volume that comes with a differentiable function that may or may not contain neural network parameters.

A convolutional neural network is composed of several subsampling and convolutional layers that are times followed by fully-connected or dense layers. As you already know, the input of a convolutional neural network is a nxnxr image where n represents the height and width of an input image while the r is a total number of channels present. The convolutional neural networks may also contain k filters known as kernels. When kernels are present, they are determined as q, which can be the same as the number of channels.

Each convolutional neural network map is subsampled with max or mean pooling over pxp of a contiguous area in which p commonly ranges between two for small images and more than 5 for larger images. Either after or before the subsampling layer a sigmoidal non-linearity and additive bias is applied to every feature map. After these convolutional neural layers, there may be several fully-connected layers and the structure of these fully-connected layers is the same as the structure of standard multilayer neural networks.

## How Convolutional Neural Networks Work?

A convolutional neural network structure of ConvNet is normally used for various deep learning problems. As already mentioned, convolutional neural networks are used for object recognition, object segmentation, detection and computer vision due to their structure. Convolutional neural networks, in fact, learn directly from image data, so there is no need to perform manual feature extraction which is commonly required in regular deep neural networks.

The use of convolutional neural networks has become popular due to three main factors. The first of them is the structure of CNNs, which eliminates the need for performing manual data extraction as all data features are learned directly by the convolutional neural networks. The second reason for the increasing popularity of convolutional neural networks is that they produce amazing, state-of-art object recognition results.

The third reason is that convolutional neural networks can be easily retained for many new object recognition tasks to help build other deep neural networks.

A CNN can contain hundreds of layers, which each learn automatically to detect many different features of an image data. In addition, filters are commonly applied to every training image at different resolutions, so the output of every convolved image is used as the input to the following convolutional layer.

The filters can also start with very simple image features like edges and brightness, so they commonly can increase the complexity of those image features which define the object as the convolutional layers progress.

Therefore, filters are commonly applied to every training image at different resolutions as the output of every convolved image acts as the input to the following convolutional layer.

Convolutional neural networks can be trained on hundreds, thousands and millions of images. When you are working with large amounts of image data and with some very complex network structures, you should use GPUs that can significantly boost the processing time required for training a neural network model.

Once you train your convolutional neural network model, you can use it in real-time applications like object recognition, pedestrian detection in ADAS or advanced driver assistance systems and many others.

**Convolutional Neural Networks Applications**

Convolutional neural networks are one of the main categories of deep neural networks which have proven to be very effective in numerous computer science areas like object recognition, object classification, and computer vision. ConvNets have been used for many years for distinguishing faces apart, identifying objects, powering vision in self-driving cars, and robots.

A ConvNet can easily recognize countless image scenes as well as suggest relevant captions. ConvNets are also able to identify everyday objects, animals or humans, as well. Lately, convolutional neural networks have also been used effectively in natural language processing problems like sentence classification.

Therefore, convolutional neural networks are one of the most important tools when it comes to machine learning and deep learning tasks. LeEnt was the very first convolutional neural network introduced that helped significantly propel the overall field of deep learning. This very first convolutional neural network was proposed by Yann LeCun back in 1988. It was primarily used for character recognition problems such as reading digits and codes.

Convolutional neural networks that are regularly used today for innumerable computer science tasks are very similar to this first convolutional neural network proposed back in 1988. Just like today's convolutional neural networks, LeNet was used for many character recognition tasks. Just like in LeNet, the standard convolutional neural networks we use today come with four main operations including convolution, ReLU non-linearity activation functions, sub-sampling or pooling and classification of their fully-connected layers.

These operations, in fact, are the fundamental steps of building every convolutional neural network. To move onto dealing with convolutional neural networks in

Python, we must get deeper into these four basic functions for a better understanding of the intuition lying behind convolutional neural networks.

As you know, every image can be easily represented as a matrix containing multiple values. We are going to use a conventional term channel where we are referring to a specific component of images. An image derived from a standards camera commonly has three channels including blue, red and green. You can imagine these images as three-2D matrices that are stacked over each other. Each of these matrices also comes with certain pixel values in the specific range zero to two hundred fifty-five.

On the other hand, if you have a grayscale image, you only get one channel as there are no colors present, just black and white. In our case here, we are going to consider grayscale images, so the example we are studying is just a single-2D matrix that represents a greyscale image. The value of each pixel contained in the matrix must range from zero to two hundred fifty-five. In this case, zero indicates a color of black while two hundred fifty-five indicates a color of white.

## *Stride And Padding*

Secondly, after specifying the depth, you also must specify the stride that you slide over the filter. When you have a stride that is one, you must move one pixel at a time. When you have a stride that is two, you can move two pixels at a time, but this produces smaller volumes of output spatially. By default, stride value is one. However, you can have bigger strides in the case when you want to come across less overlap between your receptive fields, but, as already mentioned, this will result in having smaller feature maps as you are skipping over image locations.

In the case when you use bigger strides, but you want to maintain the same dimensionality, you must use padding that surrounds your input with zeros. You can either pad with the values on the edge or with zeros. Once you get the dimensionality of your feature map that matches your input, you can move onto adding pooling layers that padding is commonly used in convolutional neural networks when you want to preserve the size of your feature maps. If you do not use padding, your feature maps will shrink at every layer. Adding zero-padding is times very convenient when you want to pad your input volume just with zeros all around the border. This is called as zero-padding which is a hyperparameter. By using zero-padding, you can control the size of your output volumes.

You can easily compute the spatial size of your output volume as a simple function of your input volume size, the convolution layers receptive field size, the stride you applied and the amount of zero-padding you used in your convolutional neural network border. For instance, if you have a 7x7 input and, if your use a 3x3 filter with stride one and pad zero, you will get a 5x5 output following the formula. If you have stride two, you will get a 3x3 output volume and so on using the formula as following in which W represents the size of your input volume, F represents the receptive field size of your convolutional neural layers, S represents the stride applied and P represents the amount of zero-padding you used.

$$(W-F +2P)/S+1$$

Using this formula, you can easily calculate how many neurons can fit in your convolutional neural network. Consider using zero-padding whenever you can. For instance, if you have an equal input and output dimensions which are five, you can use zero-padding of one to get three receptive fields. If you do not use zero-padding in the cases like this, you will get your output volume with a spatial dimension of three, as three is a number of neurons that can fit into your original input.

Spatial arrangement hypermeters commonly have mutual constraints. For instance, if you have input size of ten with no zero-padding used and with a filter size of three, it is impossible to apply stride. Therefore, you will get the set of your hyperparameter to be invalid and your convolutional neural networks library will throw an exception or zero pad completely to the rest to make it fit. Fortunately, sizing the convolutional layers properly so all dimensions included work using zero-padding can really make any job easier.

## Parameter Sharing

You can use a parameter sharing scheme in your convolutional layers to entirely control the number of used parameters. If you denoted a single two-dimensional slice of depth as your depth slice, you can constrain the neurons contained in every depth slice to use the same bias and weights. Using parameter sharing techniques, you will get a unique collection of weights, one of every depth slice, and you will get a unique collection of weights. Therefore, you can significantly reduce the number of parameters contained in the first layer of your ConvNet. Doing this step, all neurons in every depth slice of your ConvNet will use the same parameters.

In other words, during backpropagation, every neuron contained in the volume will automatically compute the gradient for all its weights.

However, these computed gradients will add up over every depth slice, so you get to update just a single collection of weights per depth slice. that all neurons contained in one depth slice will use the exact same weight vector. Therefore, when you forward pass of the convolutional layers in every depth slice, it is computed as a convolution of all neurons' weights alongside the input volume. This is the reason why we refer to the collection of weights we get as a kernel or a filter, which is convolved with your input.

However, there are a few cases in which this parameter sharing assumption, in fact, does not make any sense. This is commonly the case with many input images to a convolutional layer that come with certain centered structure, where you must learn different features depending on your image location.

For instance, when you have an input of several faces which have been centered in your image, you probably expect to get different hair-specific or eye-specific features that could be easily learned at many spatial locations. When this is the case, it is very common to just relax this parameter sharing scheme and simply use a locally-connected layer.

## Matrix Multiplication

The convolution operation commonly performs those dot products between the local regions of the input and between the filters. In these cases, a common implementation technique of the convolutional layers is to take full advantage of this fact and to formulate the specific forward pass of the main convolutional layer representing it as one large matrix multiply.

Implementation of matrix multiplication is when the local areas of an input image are completely stretched out into different columns during an operation known as im2col. For instance, if you have an input of size 227x227x3 and you convolve it with a filter of size 11x11x3 at a stride of 4, you must take blocks of pixels in size 11x11x3 in the input and stretch every block into a column vector of size 363.

However, when you iterate this process in your input stride of 4, you get fifty-five locations along both weight and height that lead to an output matrix of x col in which every column contained in fact is a maximally stretched out receptive fields and where you have 3025 fields in total.

that as the receptive fields overlap, each number in your input volume can be duplicated in multiple distinct columns. Also, remember, that the weights of the convolutional layers are very similarly stretched out into certain rows as well. For instance, if you have 95 filters in size of 11x11x3, you will get a matrix of w row of size 96x363.

When it comes to matrix multiplications, the result you get from your convolution will be equal to performing one huge matrix multiply that evaluates the dot products between every receptive field and between every filter resulting in the output of your dot production of every filter at every location. Once you get your result, you must reshape it back to its right output dimension, which in this case is 55x55x96.

This is a great approach, but it has a downside. The main downside is that it uses a lot of memory as the values contained in your input volume will be replicated several times. However, the main benefit of matrix multiplications is that there are many implementations that can improve your model. In addition, this im2col ideal can be re-used many times when you are performing pooling operation.

# Chapter 8: Machine learning

What is Machine Learning?

Now that we know a bit about data science, it is time to work a bit more with the specifics of machine learning. When it comes to looking at technology, you will find that machine learning is something that is really growing like crazy. You may not have been able to learn much about machine learning in the past, but it is likely that, even if you haven't done much in the world of technology, you have used machine learning in some form or another.

For example, you have probably used this kind of technology when you are using some kind of search engine to look up something online. Machine learning is the best option for you to use to make sure that you are able to make these search engines work for you. The program for the search engine is going to use machine learning to help the user get the search results that they need. And if it is set up in the right way, it is going to learn a bit from the choices of the user, helping it to become more accurate over time.

This is just one of the examples that you are able to see when it comes to technologies that will rely on machine learning. You will find that in addition to working on a search engine, including Google, this technology is going to work with some spam messages and some other applications. Unlike some of the traditional programs that you may have learned how to work within the past, machine learning is going to be able to make adjustments and changes based on the behavior of the user. This helps you to have more options and versatility about the programs that you create.

There are a lot of computers out there that will have machine learning already on them, and you can even program these computers in order to learn from the inputs that the user is going to give it.

### The Basics of Machine Learning

Now that we have had some time to go over a few of the basics that come with machine learning, it is time to delve in a bit more and learn how this process works, and why it is so important when you are trying to work on programs that are able to do what you want. When you are working with this kind of programming, you get the benefit of teaching a computer, or even a specific program, how to work with the experiences it has had in the past so that it can perform the way that it should in the future.

A good idea of how to illustrate this in the field is the idea of filtering out spam email. There are a few different methods that a programmer is able to use to make this one work. But one of the best and the simplest versions that you are able to work with for your program is to teach the computer how it is able to categorize, memorize, and then identify all of the different emails that are found in your inbox that you have gone through and labeled as spam. If it is successful, it should, at least most of the time, be able to tell when an email is spam and keep it out of your inbox.

While this is a memorization method that is easy to program, there are still a few things that could fail with it, and make it not work the way that you want. First, you are going to miss out on a bit of inductive reasoning in that program, which is something that must be present for efficient learning. Since you are the programmer, you will find that it is much better to go through and program the computer so that it can learn how to discern the message types that come in and that are spam, rather than trying to get the program to memorize the information.

To make sure that this process of machine learning is easy as possible, your goal would be to program the computer in a way that it is able to scan through any email that comes through the spam folder or any that it has learned is spam over time. From this scan, the program is going to be able to recognize different words and phrases that seem to be common in a message that is spam. The program could then scan through any of the newer emails that you get and have a better chance at matching up which ones should go to your inbox and which ones are spams.

You may find that this method is going to be a bit harder to program and take a bit more time, but it is a much better method to work with. You do need to take the proper precautions ahead of time with it to ensure that when the program gets things wrong (and it will make mistakes on occasion), you are able to go through and fix it fast.

There are many times that a person would be able to take a look at an email and with a glance figure out if it is spam or not. The machine learning program is going to do a pretty good job with this, but it is not perfect. You want to make sure that you are teaching it the right way to look at the emails that you get. And, sometimes, it will send perfectly good emails to the spam folder. But the more practice it gets with this and the more it learns how to work with what is spam and what isn't, the better it is going to get at this whole process.

Are there any benefits that come with machine learning?

There are a lot of different programming options that you are able to work with when it comes to making a program or doing some code. Machine learning is just one of the options that you can work with. With that said, you may be curious as to what are the benefits of working in machine learning rather than one of the other options.

At this point, you are curious as to why machine learning is going to be so great, and why you would want to make sure this is the method that you will use. There are a lot of options that you can program and code when you are working with machine learning, but we are going to focus on two main ones that are sure to make your programming needs a bit better.

The first concept that we are going to look at is the fact that machine learning means that you are able to handle any kind of task that seems too complex for a programmer to place into the computer. The second one is the idea that you are able to use the things that you learn from machine learning in order to adaptively generate all of the different tasks that you need to do. With these two concepts in mind, let's take a look at some situations where you may want to work with machine learning, where other codes and programming tricks and techniques are just not going to cut it.

## Some More Complicated Tasks

The first category that we are going to look at when it comes to using machine learning is with some of the more complicated tasks that come up. There are going to be a few tasks that you are able to work on with your programming skills that, no matter how hard you try, just seem to not mesh together with traditional coding skills. These tasks may not be able to provide a high level of clarity that traditional coding need, or they have too much in terms of complexity that comes with them.

You will find that the first category of tasks that we are going to look at here is going to be any that a person or some kind of animal would be able to perform. For example, speech recognition, driving, and even image recognition would fit into here. Humans are able to do this without even thinking, but they would be really hard to teach a program to work with, especially if you are trying to use some conventional coding techniques. But machine learning will be able to step in and make sure that this works out the way that you would like.

The next issue that you may run into when working with the idea of machine learning is that it is going to handle some tasks and concepts that a human could run into some trouble. This may include doing things like going through huge amounts of data or at least a complex type of data. There are many companies who collect data about their customers to use in the future. But if the company is big, that is a ton of data to work with.

While a person would be able to do this and maybe come up with a decent analysis, it would take forever. And by the time they got all of that data sorted through, there would probably be new data that needs some attention, and they would fall behind and be using outdated information. With machine learning, the business would be able to go through this information quickly and come up with some smart predictions that would be easy to use and promote the business forward.

You may find that you can use some of the concepts that come with machine learning to help with projects that work with genomic data, weather prediction, and search engines. There is going to be a lot of information that is seen as valuable with all of the different sets of data, but it is hard to find the time and the energy to go through this information. And it may not be done in a manner that is timely. But machine learning can step in and get it done.

If you have already spent some time learning about traditional programming and you know how to use a traditional coding language, then it is likely that you already know some of the cool things that you are able to do with them. But there are a lot of different things and things that will be more useful as technology progresses even more that machine learning will be able to help you to do.

### Adaptively Generated Tasks

You will find that conventional programs can do a lot of really cool things, but there are some limitations to watch out for. One of these limitations is that these conventional programs are a little bit rigid. Once you write out the code and implement it, the codes are going to stay the same all the time. These codes will do the same thing over and over unless the programmer changes the code, but they can't learn and adapt.

There will be times when you are working on a program that you want to act in a different manner or react to an input that it receives. Working with a conventional program will not allow this to happen. But working with machine learning allows you to work with a method that teaches the program how to change. Spam detection in your email showed a good example of how this can work.

Machine learning is easier to work with than you would think.

Yes, there are going to be some algorithms and other tasks that come with machine learning that are more complex and take some time to learn. There are a lot of examples of what is possible with machine learning that is actually pretty simple. Your projects are going to be more complicated compared to what you saw with regular programming, but machine learning is able to take those complicated tasks and make them easier. You will be surprised at how easy it is to use the programming techniques of machine learning to do some tasks like facial recognition and speech recognition.

Machine learning is often the choice to work with because it has the unique ability to learn as it goes along the process. For example, we are able to see how this works with speech recognition. Have you ever used your smartphone or another device to talk to it and had some trouble with it being able to understand you, especially in the beginning? Over time, though, the more that you were able to use the program, the better it got at being able to understand you. In the beginning, you may have had to repeat yourself over and over again, but in the end, you are able to use it any way that you would like and it will understand you. This is an example of how machine learning is able to learn your speech patterns and understand what you are saying over time.

While machine learning is going to be able to work with a lot of different actions that may be considered complex, you will find that it is really easy to work with some of the codes that go with it and you may be surprised at how a little coding can go a long way. If you have already worked with a bit of coding and programming in the past, then you will be able to catch on quick, and it won't take much longer for those who are brand new to the idea either.

What are some of the ways that I can apply machine learning?

Now that we know a bit more about the different benefits that come with machine learning, it is time to move on and learn a bit more about some of the other things that you are going to be able to do with this as well. As you start to work with the process of machine learning a bit more, you will find that there are a lot of different ways that you are able to use it and many programmers are taking it to the next level to create things that are unique and quite fun.

You may also start to notice that there are many different companies, from startups to more established firms, that are working with machine learning because they love what it is able to do to help their business grow. There are so many options when it comes to working with machine learning, but some of the ones that you may use the most often are going to include:

- Statistical research: machine learning is a big part of IT now. You will find that machine learning will help you to go through a lot of complexity when looking through large data patterns. Some of the options that will use statistical research include search engines, credit cards, and filtering spam messages.

- Big data analysis: many companies need to be able to get through a lot of data in a short amount of time. They use this data to recognize how their customers spend money and even to make decisions and predictions about the future. This used to take a long time to have someone sit through and look at the data, but now machine learning can do the process faster and much more efficiently. Options like election campaigns, medical fields, and retail stores have used machine learning for this purpose.

- Finances: some finance companies have also used machine learning. Stock trading online has seen a rise in the use of machine learning to help make efficient and safe decisions and so much more.

As we have mentioned above, these are just three of the ways that you are able to apply the principles of machine learning in order to get the results that you want to aid in your business or even to help you create a brand new program that works the way that you want. As technology begins to progress, even more, you will find that new applications and ideas for how this should work are going to grow as well.

Are there certain programs I can use machine learning with?

By now, you shouldn't be too surprised that there are a lot of different programs that you are able to utilize with machine learning, and many more are likely to be developed as time goes on. This makes it a really fun thing to learn how to work with and your options are pretty much going to be limited only by your imagination and coding skills.

There are a lot of different applications where you are able to use machine learning, and you will find that each of them can show you a different way that machine learning is going to work. Some examples of what you are able to do when you start to bring out machine learning will include:

- Search engines: A really good example of machine learning is with search engines. A search engine is going to be able to learn from the results that you push when you do a search. The first few times, it may not be as accurate because there are so many options, and you may end up picking an option that is further down the page. But as you do more searches, the program will learn what your preferences are and it can get better at presenting you with the choices that you want.

- Collaborative filtering: This is a challenge that a lot of online retailers can run into because they will use it to help them get more profits through sales. Think about when you are on a site like Amazon.com. After you do a few searches, you will then get recommendations for other products that you may want to try out. Amazon.com uses machine learning in order to figure out what items you would actually be interested in, in the hopes of helping you to make another purchase.

- Automatic translation: If you are working with a program that needs to translate things, then you are working with machine learning. The program needs to be able to look at a document and then recognize and understand the words that are there along with the syntax, grammar, and context of the words that are there. And then, if there are mistakes in the original document, this can make it harder for the program to learn along the way. The process of machine learning needs to teach the program how to translate a language from one point to another, and if it is able to do this with more than two languages, then it needs to learn all the different rules of grammar between each one. The programs that are out right now for this are still in beginner stages, so it's important that machine learning is used to improve them.

- Name recognition: Another option that you are able to use with machine learning is the idea of name identity recognition. This is when the program is set up so that it will recognize different entities including places, actions, and names when it is reading through a document. You will be able to work with a program and ask it to digest and then comprehend the information that it reads. This helps to find the information that is in the document much faster than you have to read through it all.

- Speech recognition: We talked about this one a bit before. But you will find that speech recognition is a great example of how you are able to work with machine learning. Speech recognition is going to be a hard thing to work with. There are so many speech patterns, differences between ages and genders, and even languages and dialects that it is hard to make any kind of program that will do well with recognizing the speech patterns of those who talk to it. But since machine learning can learn as it goes through the process, you get the benefit of having it get more familiar with your way of talking. There are going to be some mistakes and issues along the way. But if you are able to work with it and get through those early stages, the program will be able to learn and you get the benefit of getting a program that understands your requests.

- Facial recognition: And the final thing that we are going to take a look at is the idea of facial recognition. This is where the program is going to be able to look at the face of a person and recognize who they are. Or at least it will be able to tell if that person has security clearance to be in a certain area, for example. It is going to go through a series of learning processes in order to tell who is able to be on the system and who should be turned away in the process.

- There are so many cool things that you are able to do when you start to bring in some machine learning. And while all of these sound hard and would be nearly impossible with the conventional forms of programming, you will find that they can be easy and a lot of fun to work with when you are doing machine learning.

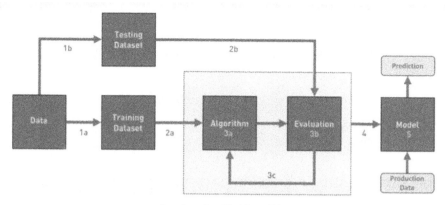

Overview of the Workflow of ML

141

# Chapter 9: Importance of data science in job and business

What is Data Science?

The term Data Science is common nowadays, but what does it mean? What skills does a person need to have to be called a Data Scientist? How are predictions and decisions made in Data Science? Is there a difference between Data Science and Business Intelligence? These are some of the questions that you are going to find answers to in a short while.

First, let's define Data Science.

Data Science refers to a combination of several tools, Machine Learning principles, and algorithms whose purpose is to discover hidden patterns from raw data. One might wonder how different it is from Statistics. The figure below has all the answers.

The figure above shows that a Data Analyst explains whatever is happening by processing history of the data. On the other hand, a Data Scientist will not only explain to extract insights from it, but they will also use different advanced Machine Learning algorithms to highlight the occurrence of a specific event in the future. A Data Scientist looks at the data from different perspectives and angles.

If you need a model that has the intelligence and capability to make its own decisions, then prescriptive analytics is the best to use.

This new field delivers advice; it doesn't just predict, but it also recommends different prescribed actions and related outcomes. The best example to illustrate this is the Google self-driving car. Data that is collected by the vehicle is used to train the cars. You can further mine this data by using algorithms to reveal intelligence. This will allow your car to make decisions such as when to turn, which path to take, as well as when to speed up or slow down.

• Machine Learning for Pattern Discovery. Let's say that you don't have resources that you can apply to make predictions; it will require you to determine the hidden patterns in the data set to predict correctly. The most popular algorithm applied in pattern discovery is Clustering. Assume that you work in a telephone company, and you want to determine a network by installing towers in the region. Therefore, you may use the clustering technique to determine the tower location that will make sure all users have the maximum signal strength.

- Make Predictions with Machine Learning. If you want to build a model that can predict the future trend of a company, then Machine Learning algorithms are the best to go with. This falls under supervised learning; it is called supervised because data is already present that you can use to train machines.

Data Science and Discovery of Data Insight
involves unearthing hidden insight that can allow companies to make smart business decisions. For example:

- Highlighting key customer segments inside its base as well as special shopping behaviors in the segments. This directs messages to different market audiences.

- Netflix extracts data from movie viewing patterns to find out what drives user interest and uses it to make decisions.
- Proctor and Gamble make use of time series models to understand future demand. This allows a person to plan for production levels.

But how do Data Scientists extract data insights?

If you ever asked yourself this question, the answer is: it begins with data exploration. When faced with a difficult question, Data Scientists become curious. They attempt to find leads and understand characteristics within the data. To achieve this, an individual must have a higher level of creativity.

In addition, they may choose to use quantitative techniques to move deeper. Some examples are time series forecasting, inferential models segmentation analysis, synthetic control experiments, and many more. The aim is to put together a forensic view of what the data means. Hence, data-driven insight is the key in delivering strategic guidance. In other words, the role of Data Scientists is to guide business stakeholders so that they can learn how to respond to findings.

Development of a Data Product

A data product refers to a technical asset which makes use of data as input and processes the data to display the results of an algorithm. A classic example of a data product is a recommendation engine which takes user data and builds a personalized recommendation depending on the data. Below are examples of data products:

- A computer vision applied in self-driving cars
- Gmail's spam filter
- Amazon recommendation engine

This is not similar to "data insights" discussed previously where the final result is to generate advice to an executive team to help them make better business decisions. Conversely, a data product has a technical functionality that includes an algorithm and is developed to be encapsulated directly into the major applications. Some of the popular examples of applications that have a data product working behind the scenes are:

- Amazon's home page
- Gmail's inbox
- Autonomous driving software

Data Scientists play a major role in creating a product. This includes coming up with algorithms, testing, technical deployment, and refinement. In this case, Data Scientists act as technical developers who build assets which can be leveraged at a wide view.

Requisite Skillset for a Data Scientist

Mathematics Ability

At the center of mining data insight and developing a data product is the potential to see data through a quantitative lens. There are correlations, textures, and dimensions in data that one can represent mathematically. Developing solutions that make use of data involves heuristics and quantitative techniques.

Answers to most business problems include building analytic models that are grounded in the complex math where it is important to understand the principle behind the models.

Another misconception spread by people is that Data Science is mainly Statistics. Even though Statistics is critical in Data Science, it is not the only type of math learned. There are two categories of Statistics namely Bayesian Statistics and Classical Statistics. Most people tend to refer to Classical Statistics when they speak about stats. However, one is required to have knowledge of both types of Statistics. For instance, a common method to determine hidden characteristics in a data set is the SVD. This method is rooted in matrix math and has little to do with the classical stats. In general, it is good for Data Scientists to have both breadth and depth of mathematics knowledge.

Strong Business Acumen

It is good for a Data Scientist to have the traits of a tactical business consultant. By working alone with data, they have the edge to discover new concepts from data in ways that no one can. As a result, they have the task to translate observations that they see into a shared knowledge and recommend strategies in which they can solve major business problems. Therefore, a Data Scientist should be able to use data to create a story. The story has to be a cohesive narrative of the problem and solution.

Technology and Hacking

Hacking, in this case, refers to the creativity and ingenuity in the application of technical skills to define intelligent solutions to problems.

The ability to hack is important because Data Scientists make use of technology to amass massive data sets and work with advanced algorithms. This will need advanced tools rather than Excel. A Data Scientist has to develop quick solutions and integrate them with complicated data systems. The main languages linked with Data Science include SAS, Python, and R. Other languages include Julia and Java.

However, it is not just mastering the language that is the key. A hacker should be able to solve technical challenges creatively so that a program code can function correctly.

Furthermore, a Data Science hacker should have a solid understanding of the algorithm. They can break down difficult and messy problems so that they become solvable. This is very important because Data Scientists work in an environment of complex algorithms. Therefore, they should have a strong mindset to understand complex data.

## Data Scientist – Curiosity and Training

The Mindset

A popular trait of most Data Scientists is that they think deep and have an intense intellectual curiosity. Data Science calls for one to be inquisitive. An individual has to regularly ask new questions, make new discoveries, and learn new things.

In fact, it is not money that drives them in their job but the ability to use their creativity to come up with solutions to problems and frequently engage in their curiosity. Extracting high dimensional leads from data goes just beyond making an observation. Instead, it is all about discovering the truth hidden beneath the surface. Data Scientists are grateful and passionate about what they do and find great satisfaction in taking on a challenge.

Training

There is a popular misconception that to be a certified Data Scientist, you must have a Ph.D. This view fails to consider that Data Science is multidisciplinary.

With increasing compute power and big data, deep learning is becoming key part or popular for various kind of tasks. The main reason for its popularity is that it is powered by massive amount of data and hence, we are able to achieve the results, that no other machine learning tool can provide. As there is so much data today, we can use deep learning to train our models and achieve better results than any traditional machine learning algorithms. Deep learning so, there is no need for an expert to do manual work of feature extraction. Deep learning algorithms automatically learn high level features from data. Recent advances in deep learning have reached to the point where these models surpass humans in tasks like object classification in images.

There are some quite complex tasks e.g. recognizing cat faces in variety of deformed and transformed images. It will be really hard to extract HOG features of different cat faces and using kernels from traditional computer vision to match and find cat faces in the image. With deep learning, we just have to provide labelled data and models can automatically extract and learn important features. This gives immense power to the domain of deep learning because we can now apply it to any task without worrying about extracting important features from data (which require domain experts). With the availability of huge amounts of data and with the compute power of GPUs, deep learning models can be trained on terabytes of data in a few hours using GPU clusters and cloud computing.

The idea of applying deep learning is simple but there are several complications within e.g. initialization, activations, hyperparameters etc., that makes it complex to achieve target results and hence, there is a lot of room for creative ideas in this domain.

Biological Inspiration

Human brain is the primary motivator for neural networks and deep learning. Artificial Neural networks(ANNs) are inspired by the idea of neuron firing and activation in brain. These networks are based on how humans learn and process the information. Our memory and all of our actions are controlled through our nervous system, which is composed of neurons. These neurons are connected in various ways with relative strengths. This same concept is applied in

Artificial Neural Networks. On the basic level, an artificial neural network is a bunch of artificial neurons, called perceptrons, connected together that mimic biological neurons in a brain. An artificial neuron is essentially a mathematical function applied to an input signal or value. These artificial neurons interact by passing information to other connected artificial neurons. They are organized as layers in hierarchical structure. Neurons in each layer are connected to neurons in the next layer (as shown in figure below). A neural network contains an input layer to get input data feed, a hidden layer to process that data and an output layer to provide the output. A neural network with multiple hidden layers will be called a deep neural network, hence the term, deep learning.

Although, we haven't been able to know exactly, how the human brain works but most of the concepts and ideas used in deep learning or neural networks are directly inspired from biology. For example, this hierarchy of layers in Artifical Neural Networks (ANNs) are analogous to visual streams in Broddman areas in the brain, receptive field of convolutional neurons emulate biological receptive field, suppression models are analogous to surround suppression to enable detection of object edges and shapes.

These algorithms do not perfectly emulate brain and we haven't been able to match the complexity of brain yet but still, these algorithms perform amazingly well on complex tasks. This is an active area of research in neuroscience to further understand visual cognition and information processing in brain e.g. how biological neurons perceive and process information, what events fire them the most and which parts of the brain are active at what time.

Brief history of Machine Learning/ Deep Learning

The history of deep learning can be traced back to 1943, when Warren McCulloch and Walter Pitts published a paper with a concept of Artificial Neuron(AN) to mimic the thought process. This Artificial neuron was based on the characteristic of a biological neuron of either being fully active to a stimulation or none at all. This behavior of biological neuron was observed in microelectrode readings from brain.

In 1957, Frank and Rosenblatt presented Mark I Perceptron Machine as the first implementation of perceptron algorithm. The idea was to resemble the working of biological neuron to create an agent that can learn. This perceptron was a supervised binary linear classifier with adjustable weights. This functionality was implemented through following function:

Where, w is weights vector, X is inputs and b is bias.

For each input and output pair, this formula provided classification results. If the result/prediction did not match with output, the weight vector was updated through:

Where, is predicted/output of function, is actual output, is input vector and is weight vector.

It should be noted that back at that time, they implemented this functionality through a hardware machine with wires and connections (as shown in figure below).

In 1960, Widrow and Hoff stacked these perceptrons and built a 3-layered (input layer, hidden layer, output layer), fully connected, feed-forward architecture for classification as a hardware implementation, called

ADALINE. The architecture presented in paper is shown in image below.

In 1960, Henry J. Kelley introduced continuous back propagation model, which is currently used in learning weights of the model. In 1962, a simpler version of backpropagation based on chain rule was introduced by Stuart Dreyfus but these methods were inefficient.

The backpropagation currently used in models was actually presented in 1980s.

In 1979, Fukushima designed a multi-layered convolutional neural network architecture, called Neocognitron, that could learn to recognize patterns in images. The network resembled to current day architectures but wasn't exactly the same. It also allowed to manually adjust the weight of certain connections. Many concepts from Neocognitron continue to be used. The layered connections in perceptrons allowed to develop a variety of neural networks. For several patterns present in the data, Selective Attention Model could distinguish and separate them.

In 1970, Seppo Linnainmaa presented automatic differentiation to efficiently compute the derivative of a differentiable composite function using chain rule. Its application, later in 1986, led to backpropagation of errors in multilayer perceptrons. This was when Geoff Hinton, Williams and Rumelhart presented a paper to demonstrate that backpropagation in neural networks provide interesting distribution representations. In 1989, Yann LeCun, currently, Director of AI Research Facebook, provided first practical demonstration of backpropagation in convolutional neural networks to read handwritten digits at Bell Labs. Even though with backpropagation, deep neural networks were not being able to train well.

In 1995, Vapnik and Cortes introduced support vector machines for regression and classification of data. In 1997, Schmidhuber and Hochreiter introduced Long Short Term Memory (LSTM) for recurrent neural networks.

In all these years, a major hindering constraint was compute but in 1999, computers started to become faster at processing data and Graphical Processing Units (GPUs) were introduced. This immensely increased the compute power.

In 2006, Hinton and Salakhutdinov presented a paper that reinvigorated research in deep learning. This was the first time when a proper 10 layer convolutional neural network was trained properly. Instead of training 10 layers using backpropagation, they came up with unsupervised pre-training scheme, called Restricted Boltzmann Machine. This was a 2 step approach for training. In the first step, each layer of the network was trained using unsupervised objective. In the second step, all the layers were stacked together for backpropagation.

Later in 2009, Fei-Fei Li, a professor at Stanford university launched ImageNet, a large visual database designed for visual object recognition research containing more than 14 million hand-annotated images of 20,000 different object categories. This gave neural networks a huge edge as data of this order made it possible to train neural networks and achieve good results.

In 2010, neural networks got a lot of attention from research community when Microsoft presented a paper on speech recognition and neural networks performed really well compared to other machine learning tools like SVMs and kernels. Specifically, they introduced neural network as a part of GMM and HMM framework and achieved huge improvements.

In 2012, a paper by Krizhevsky, Sutskever and Hinton showed that huge improvements are achieved through deep learning in visual recognition domain. Their model, AlexNet outperformed all the other traditional computer vision methods in visual recognition task and won several international competitions. Since then, the field has exploded and several network architectures and ideas have been introduced like GANs.

# Chapter 10:

# Data Science and its applications

## *The Art of Data Science*

When it comes to data analysis, it is not as easy as it looks. One of the reasons why it is difficult is because only a few people have mastered the art of data analysis. This means that only a few people can explain how it is done.

Surprisingly, many people try to analyze data daily, but the majority fails in their efforts. This is because experts in this field haven't taken time to explain how they think while analyzing data.

Data Science is an art. It is not a concept that one can teach a computer. Data analysts use different tools to achieve their task, right from linear regression to classification trees. Even though all these tools are known to the computer, it is the role of the data analyst to figure out a way in which he or she can gather all the tools and integrate them to data to develop the correct answer to a question.

However, the process of data analysis has not been written down properly. While there are many books written about Statistics, none of them tries to address how one can create a real-world data analysis solution. On the other hand, coming up with an important framework involves classifying elements of data analysis using an abstract language. In some cases, this language might be mathematics. Conversely, the same details of the analysis are what make each analysis complex and interesting.

The Cycle of Analysis

You might look at data analysis and think that it follows a linear, step-by-step process that has a well-developed result. However, data analysis is an iterative and non-linear approach that is depicted by a series of epicycles. In this approach, information is learned at each step which then decides whether to redo and refine the next step that is already performed or proceed to the next step.

When it comes to analyzing data, the iterative process is used in all steps of the data analysis. Besides this, certain data analysis might appear fixed and linear because of the algorithms encapsulated in the different software.

Therefore, it is important that one understand what it means by the term "data analysis". Although a study of data involves creating and implementing a plan for gathering data, data analysis assumes that data is already gathered. Most importantly, a study will involve the creation of a hypothesis, designing of a data collection procedure, gathering of data, and interpretation of the data. However, since data analysis assumes that data should be collected already, it involves the development and refinement of a question and process of analyzing and interpreting data.

There are Five Major Activities of Data Analysis:

1. State and refine the question
2. Explore the data
3. Create formal statistical models
4. Interpret the results
5. Communicate the results

All the above activities happen on different occasions. For instance, it is possible to go through all of them in a day but handle each in detail in a period of more than one month. So, let's look at the overall framework applied in each of these activities.

While there are many different types of activities that one can engage in while performing data analysis, each aspect of the whole process can be undertaken through an interactive process. Most importantly, for each of the above five activities, it is advised that you include the following steps:

1.   Define or set the expectations

2.   Collect information and compare the data to your expectations

3.   If the data fails to match your expectations, revise or fix the data so that both your expectations and data match

Going through all the three steps above is what is referred to as the cycle of the data analysis. While you navigate through every stage of the analysis, you will be required to go through the epicycle to constantly revise your question, formal models, interpretation, and communication. A repeated cycle through each of these five major activities forms the largest part of data analysis.

## Define the Expectations

In this step, you intentionally lay down what you expect before you can do anything such as performing a procedure, inspecting your data or typing a command. For the experienced data analyst, creating expectations might be automatic or a subconscious process. Despite this, it is important to think about it. For instance, if you are going to shop with friends and you have to stop by an ATM to withdraw some money, you need to decide on the amount of money that you want to withdraw. You need to have some expectations of the price of the things you are going to buy. This could be something that you have no problem with if you know the price/s of the product/s you are going to buy. This is an example of prior knowledge. Another example of prior knowledge would be to know the time that a specific restaurant closes. Using that information, you can schedule your time and activities so that you show up for dinner before it closes.

You can also find out additional information from your friends that will help you come up with expectations or Google a restaurant to learn more about their working hours. This procedure that you apply on prior information to develop expectation or implement an analysis procedure is the same used in every main activity of the analysis process.

Information Collection

This step requires one to collect information related to the question or data. For questions, one collects information by doing a literature research or finding out from experts. For the data, once you have developed some expectations about what the result can be when the data is inspected, it is okay to go ahead and carry out the operation. The results of this activity include data that you need to collect and determine whether the collected data matches your expectations.

Comparison of Expectations

Once you have the data in your hands, the next step is to compare your expectations to the data. Here, there are two possible results:

1. Your cost estimations match the amount on the check

2. Your cost estimations fail to match

If both the cost estimations and amount match, then you can move on to the next activity. Alternatively, if your expectations cost 60 dollars, but the check is 30 dollars, then your expectations and data are different. In this case, there could be two possible reasons for the difference: the first is that you may have wrong expectations and you need to revise; and second, the check may be wrong and contains errors. One key indicator that can hint on the status of your data analysis is the easiness or difficultness to match the data you collected to your original expectations.

Volume, Velocity, and Variety

Big Data has various "V"s. The major ones include velocity, variety, and volume. Big Data surpasses the storage capacity of normal databases. The scale of data generated is massive. As of today, a huge amount of data is generated. One reason for this is because of the increase in interaction. Interaction is a new phenomenon besides just transaction of data. Data interaction comes from activities of the browser, personal digital recorders, and geo-location.

With the advent of the "internet of things", massive data is produced that humans spend their entire time trying to analyze.

A good Data Scientist should know how to control volume. He or she should know how to create algorithms that can intelligently use the size of the data effectively. Things acquire a new direction when you have gargantuan data because each similarity becomes important, and one can easily make false conclusions. In most business applications, extraction of correlation is enough. However, the right Data Science uses techniques that determine the cause based on these correlations.

Data velocity will always accelerate. There is an increase in Facebook posts, tweets, and financial information generated by many users at a higher speed. Velocity increases the volume of data and reduces the time of data retention. For example, a high-frequency trading activity depends on data streams and fast information. But the authenticity of the data reduces rapidly.

Lastly, data variety has gone deep. Models which depend on just a handful of variables can now produce hundreds of variables because of the increase in computing power. The rate of change in volume, velocity, and data variety is currently possible for new economic-metrics and various tools.

Machine Learning

Machine Learning refers to how systems learn from various types of data they process. It is possible to train a system based on particular data to make decisions. The training process occurs continuously to enable systems to make updates and enhance decision-making ability. Systems that use spam filters are a great example to demonstrate how Machine Learning is applied. These systems use a Bayesian filter to change decisions.

Therefore, it will continue to stay ahead of spammers. The ability to dynamically learn is important because it helps prevent spammers from gaming the filter. Credit approvals use neural-nets and are a great example of Machine Learning technique. Besides that, Machine

Learning prefers data compared to judgments. Hence, a good Data Scientist should have a variety of both. Machine Learning has helped in finding answers to questions of interest, and it has further proved to be a game-changer. What makes Machine Learning very interesting is the four characteristics of machine intelligence:

1.      It is built on a strong foundation of a theoretical breakthrough

2.      It redefines the current economic paradigm

3.      The final result is commoditization

4.      It unearths new data from Data Science


Supervised and Unsupervised Learning


There are two broad ways that a system can learn: supervised and unsupervised learning.

Supervised learning is where a system makes decisions depending on the type of data entered. Automated credit card approvals and spam filters apply supervised learning to achieve their functions. The system is supplied with a historical data sample of outputs and inputs. Based on this type of data, the system establishes the relationship between the two using Machine Learning techniques. You will need to use your judgment to choose the best technique to handle the task.

Unsupervised learning happens when you only have input data (X) without a corresponding output variable. Unsupervised learning aims to build a model of the underlying structure in the data order so that you can learn more about the data. It is called unsupervised learning because there is no correct answer and teacher. Algorithms are left to decide and discover interesting structure in the data.

Cluster analysis is an example of unsupervised learning. Cluster analysis selects a group of entities each with a different attribute and divides the entity space based on how far or near the entities of the attributes are. This will rearrange and redefine data by labeling it using additional tags. Factor analysis is part of the unsupervised learning technique.

Predictions and Forecasts

Data Science involves making forecasts and predictions. However, there is a distinction between the two. Predictions focus on highlighting a single outcome. If a person says that "it will be cold tomorrow," he or she has predicted. But if they say that "the chance of tomorrow being cold is 40%," they shall have made a forecast. This is because a forecast provides outcomes in the form of probabilities.

# Conclusion

I hope this book has provided you with all the tools you need to achieve your goals.

The next step is to get started using the new skills that you learned about data science. Data science is a newer field of study that many businesses are quickly learning is important in helping them out. When it is combined with knowledge and experience in a specific industry, it can be one of the best ways to ensure that you make great and profitable business decisions. Going through all the data on your own, especially if it is large, can be a challenge sometimes. But data science shows you the different methods that you can use to get this done quickly and efficiently.

This guidebook has gone over the basics of what you need to know to get started with data science. We looked at what data science is, what it can be used for, some of the different techniques that you can use with it, and even how to work with the algorithms and the data modeling of some of your projects.

Now, you should be well on your way to understanding what data science is and how you can use it in your own business to make great business decisions.

When you are ready to collect and analyze large amounts of data for your company, and use it to learn more about your business and your customers, make sure to refer to this guidebook.